subversive Jesus Radical Grace

RELATING CHRIST TO A NEW GENERATION

ROBERT THORNTON HENDERSON

NAVPRESS

Bringing Truth to Life
P.O. Box 35001, Colorado Springs, Colorado 80935

OUR GUARANTEE TO YOU

We believe so strongly in the message of our books that we are making this quality guarantee to you. If for any reason you are disappointed with the content of this book, return the title page to us with your name and address and we will refund to you the list price of the book. To help us serve you better, please briefly describe why you were disappointed. Mail your refund request to: NavPress, P.O. Box 35002, Colorado Springs, CO 80935.

The Navigators is an international Christian organization. Our mission is to reach, disciple, and equip people to know Christ and to make Him known through successive generations. We envision multitudes of diverse people in the United States and every other nation who have a passionate love for Christ, live a lifestyle of sharing Christ's love, and multiply spiritual laborers among those without Christ.

NavPress is the publishing ministry of The Navigators. NavPress publications help believers learn biblical truth and apply what they learn to their lives and ministries. Our mission is to stimulate spiritual formation among our readers.

© 2001 by Robert Thornton Henderson
All rights reserved. No part of this publication may be reproduced in any form without written permission from NavPress, P.O. Box 35001, Colorado Springs, CO 80935.
www.navpress.com
Library of Congress Catalog Card Number: 2001030057
ISBN 1-57683-277-5

Cover design by Dan Jamison
Cover digital photography by Nanette Hoogslag / Digital Vision
Creative team: Don Simpson, Greg Clouse, Marla Kennedy, Pat Miller

Some of the anecdotal illustrations in this book are true to life and are included with the permission of the persons involved. All other illustrations are composites of real situations, and any resemblance to people living or dead is coincidental.

Unless otherwise identified, all Scripture quotations in this publication are taken from the *HOLY BIBLE: NEW INTERNATIONAL VERSION*® (NIV). Copyright © 1973, 1978, 1984 by International Bible Society. Used by permission of Zondervan Publishing House. All rights reserved. All other versions are author translations, paraphrases, or amalgams of several translations and commentaries.

Henderson, Robert T., 1928-
   Subversive Jesus, radical grace : relating Christ to a new generation / Robert Thornton Henderson.
      p. cm.
   Includes bibliographical references.
   ISBN 1-57683-277-5
      1. Evangelistic work. 2. Church work with youth. 3. Church work with young adults. 4. Generation X—Religious life. I. Title.

BV4447.H38 2001
243—dc21

2001030057

Printed in the United States of America

1 2 3 4 5 6 7 8 9 10 / 05 04 03 02 01

FOR A FREE CATALOG OF
NAVPRESS BOOKS & BIBLE STUDIES,
CALL 1-800-366-7788 (USA)
OR 1-416-499-4615 (CANADA)

Table of Contents

Preface

There is no doubt in my mind that the title of this book will initially be misunderstood, if not actually rankle many would-be readers. Yet in no way am I attempting to be clever or stir up controversy. My use of the word subversive is prompted by some thoughts of the late French sociologist-theologian Jacques Ellul in his seminal book, *The Subversion of Christianity*. In it he explains that the rebellion of the creation against the Creator was, first of all, a subversion of God's design, and goes on to suggest that the work of Jesus was to subvert the subversion! Jesus came to inaugurate a whole New Creation, a new and radically different dominion, which he preached as the gospel of the kingdom of God.[1] In this sense, and to use contemporary political terms, Jesus came to engage in counterinsurgency.

So, that is my rationale for designating Jesus as a *subversive*.

As to my use of the word *radical*, it is also by design because it means getting to the *root* or the basic principle of a thing. When you explore God's *grace*, right away you have to ask what is the ultimate purpose of that grace, and what is it that God sovereignly intends, in his mercy and grace, to see occur. You come to the conclusion that it is to make all things new! It is the New Creation in which the whole of creation once again reflects the glory of the Creator. This is *radical* if that word has any meaning at all!

The very fact that Jesus comes with such a redemptive and subversive agenda, and that his grace is committed to whatever it takes to make this a reality, disturbs our comfort zone. It makes demands upon us. It calls for change and cleansing and for unknowns. At the same time, it surfaces the reality that in much of popular evangelicalism there has been what I have to charitably believe to be an inadvertent reductionism in the presentation of the gospel. I am always fascinated by my evangelical friends who are so gifted in presenting the incredible promises of the gospel and making God's love so compelling. Everything they say is true and needs to be heralded. It is not what they say that leaves me with a lurking sense that something is wrong. It is what they do *not* say.

Matthew's account of Christ's great commission presents the mandate to make disciples among all the people-groups of the world. But it goes on to define what that involves and, along with baptism, is the telling piece that so often gets left out: "teaching them to obey everything I have commanded you."[2] I am reminded of Jesus' illustration in the Sermon on the Mount of the person who builds his house on the rock as being the one who "has these words of mine and *does* them" (emphasis added).[3] In Luke's account of the Great Commission, he emphasizes that "repentance and the forgiveness of sins be preached in his name in every people-group."[4] The word *repentance* carries with it the idea of total transformation of mind by which we forsake one way of life and enter into another. It is the threshold of Jesus' invitation to leave the dominion of darkness and enter into the dominion of God's dear Son, and this totally by God's grace. In other words, God is willing to do what is necessary to make it happen despite what we may deserve. Radical!

God does indeed want all men and women everywhere to find his salvation. But when the gospel is truncated so that the focus on his promises mutes or obfuscates the call to new obedience, then some tragedy happens. The gospel is subverted. And we find in North America (and elsewhere) a very large "evangelical establishment" that hardly evidences any difference from the secular community around it, and has little enlightening or leavening effect on the world.

And so I offer this book as a door back into a gospel that has transformational dimensions.

Two Necessary Explanations

1. Jesus, in the three synoptic gospels (Matthew, Mark, and Luke), uses the term "gospel of the kingdom" almost

universally as his description of the gospel. This makes our understanding of the kingdom of God to be somewhat critical. My assumption is that Jesus came to announce and inaugurate the kingdom of God. My assumption is that he did on the cross what was necessary to effect a reconciliation between God and sinful humanity, and to offer those wonderful promises of forgiveness and full atonement. I also assume that radical grace didn't leave it alone at that point, but that Jesus, by the presence of the Holy Spirit, now makes the kingdom of God dynamically present and active, and is creating a community of the kingdom known as the church. Further, I assume that there is before us the second advent of Christ when he shall return in power and great glory, and the kingdom of God shall be consummated in all of its fullness. Or as Paul states it:

> "Then the end will come, when he hands over
> the kingdom to God the Father after he has
> destroyed all dominion, authority and power.
> For he must reign until he has put all his ene-
> mies under his feet. The last enemy to be
> destroyed is death. . . .When he has done this,
> then the Son himself will be made subject to
> him who put everything under him, so that
> God may be all in all."[5]

This frequently is described as *the-already-but-not-yet-kingdom.*

2. My continual assumption is that several New Testament designations are all nuanced terms referring to the same reality. They are: *the kingdom of God* (which I fairly regularly translate as *dominion of God* because North Americans haven't figured out kings and kingdoms very well), *salvation, eternal life, New Creation, the age to*

come, righteousness, reconciliation, redemption, and
Shalom. I see these terms as facets, or different windows,
into God's great purpose in Christ. In all of them we are
looking at the sovereign good purpose of God to reconcile heaven and earth through Jesus Christ. I will without explanation beyond this point interplay these terms.

AN IMPOSSIBLE TASK?

With such a plethora of books on evangelism, it seems presumptuous to write another. But as we move into a totally new (postmodern) culture that is vigorously secular and pagan, and therefore
biblically and theologically illiterate, there is emerging the awareness of a vast and unmet spiritual hungering. For this reason, I have
written in a semi-dialogical fashion with a person from Generation
X and his successor, a person from Generation Y, looking over my
shoulder. We will also witness a conversation with three newly
found friends who are followers of Jesus. Gen X'ers (those born
between 1964 and 1981) and Gen Y'ers, or Millennials or Net
Gen'ers as they're commonly called (those born between 1982 and
2000), are the next great mission field, and they tug at my heart in
a compelling way.

All of this is made more interesting as we face the culture's
increasing hostility toward any remnant of Christian hegemony.
Ours is an age suspicious of words and cynical about any religious
claims. Jesus becomes the butt of crude jokes. There is nothing
holy, no moral boundaries. Sullenness is everywhere, along with a
hyperactive frenzy to make sense of it all.

In all of this I am so very indebted to those friends with whom
I resonate in this concern, and who have enriched me by their
insights and encouragements. May the Holy Spirit, the Spirit of
the Father and the Son, make these words a ministry for equipping
his faithful church.

All praise to the Lamb of God!

ONE

Jesus in a "Yeah, Right!" Culture

Is there anything out there, any meaning, any hope? What is life all about?

—Chip

Question: How are outsiders (the unchurched, or just normal secular modern, or more likely, postmodern folk) attracted to the Christian message and the point of inquiry? How do we attract them in the midst of a cynical and word-weary culture bombarded with all kinds of religious hustles? Not to mention all the stuff that parades under the name of Jesus that is, frankly, an embarrassment. Our friends outside are likely to respond: "Yeah, right! So. . . ?"

How does a thoughtful Christian, or Christian congregation, cope with this insistent and complicating cultural reality? What do we do with the disturbing fact that while the Christian church in the United States is at a higher profile than ever, the country devolves morally and ethically more and more into a neo-pagan darkness, without absolutes?

At a different level, what are we to make of the all-too-frequent abandonment by Christians of the eroding American urban scene, or of the public school system, both of which are major missionary contexts? Or what of the Christians' response to the environmental dilemma? Or, closer to home, what are we inside the church to make of our embarrassing capitulation to the grosser forms of consumerism?

Good questions!

Yet all of this takes place when right under our noses is emerging a younger generation that lives with an intense spiritual hungering and not a clue what it is or where to turn to satisfy it.

A Story

Consider the following story that began one Sunday morning at All Saints Episcopal Church. It started with an incidental and friendly contact and developed into an ongoing conversation. It became, I suppose you could say, an evangelistic dialogue in the truest sense of the term. It involved several friends, but our focus is especially on Chip. A member of the church named Kate had noticed this young guy enter the sanctuary late and look around somewhat uncertainly. He slid into the end of the pew a few feet from her. As is often true with anyone unfamiliar with the Episcopal service, he fumbled between an unfamiliar order of worship and more unfamiliar *Book of Common Prayer*, not knowing when to kneel and when to sit. So Kate moved next to him, smiled, and offered to share her book with him. A bit embarrassed, he accepted.

He sat there taking it all in. He checked out the stained glass windows, scoped out the congregation, and often wrinkled his brow trying to comprehend the words of the priest. After the closing ascription, Kate introduced herself and asked, "You're new here, aren't you?" To which Chip responded, "Is it that obvious?" They laughed. "What did you think of it all?" she asked.

"Honestly?"

"Yes, honestly."

"Totally, like totally, confusing. So much stuff doesn't make any sense. Even contradictory."

Subversive Jesus, Radical Grace

"Like what, for instance?"

"Well, for starters, I don't even remotely relate to stuff like straying sheep, and sin, merciful fathers, all of that."

"Okay, and what about the contradictory part?"

"Well maybe I missed something, but it sure sounds like somebody talking out of both sides of his mouth. We read all that stuff in the book about being joyful in the Lord and heartily rejoicing in God, and all of that, then the guy up there begins reading about people reviling you, persecuting you, and saying all kinds of bad stuff about you. He even read from somewhere that Christian people shouldn't think it too weird when fiery trials come down. Like, gimme a break! What's going on? God loves me, but if I follow him I get fiery trials and persecutions? Yeah, right! Hey! I've got enough problems in my life without any of that. I'm already in over my head without that kind of prospect. I don't mean to be nasty about it, but get real! Hey, you asked!"

"Uh-huh! Good point. Does sound sort of like doublespeak, doesn't it? I think there may be a bit more here than meets the eye, but that's a longer story. How would you feel about pursuing this conversation a bit further?" Kate dangled the invitation in front of Chip.

"Why not? When? Where?"

"I'll tell you what. I live not too far away, and a few of my fun friends, neat people, are coming over to my place this evening for lasagna, and they'd love to be in on the conversation too. They are, I must warn you, all Christians—you know, followers of Jesus—but they're a laid-back bunch who'd love to meet you and process these confusions with us. OK?"

"Cool!"

So with time and place arranged, the dinner party unfolded.

HONESTY, INQUIRY, AND LASAGNA

Late that afternoon Chip found his way to Kate's condo. Barbara and Jong—young adult neighbors in the complex, and both employed by the same company headquarters in Midtown—had already arrived.

Once introductions were complete and everyone was digging into chips and dip on the coffee table, Chip dug right in too. "So all of you guys are really into this Christian thing, right?" They smiled at his candor. Acknowledging that such was the case, they waited for his next comment. "Hey! It could make a guy feel like this deck is stacked, but then again, what do I have to lose? Thanks for letting me come and spill my own confusion on you." There was an interesting mixture of blunt honesty and winsomeness in Chip—and, as they would soon find, a large streak of cynicism too.

When dinner was on the table and they were seated, Kate prayed and thanked God for the food and friends. Chip didn't quite know what had just happened, but whatever it was, it didn't seem to disturb his anticipation of the aromatic lasagna and the equally attractive tossed salad in front of him. They were on their way. Lots of friendly banter and reporting on the week's activities. Chip seemed at home in the conversations, being an environmental engineer by training, and well informed on all manner of cultural happenings, media, and sports events. When the babble came to a point where it could be interrupted, Kate reported on her meeting with Chip after church, and his questions, confusion, and perception of contradictions. "It seemed to me a pretty honest appraisal, and worth pursuing. I'm glad you guys could come and process it with us."

Kate proposed that everybody take a few minutes to tell something about their lives, and some evaluation of their response to Jesus Christ—both positive and negative. She had hardly gotten the proposal out of her mouth when Chip volunteered to go first because he was obviously the guy who initiated all of this by showing up at Kate's church that particular morning.

Chip

Chip's story was heartbreakingly similar to many of his generation. His parents were ambitious Boomers into their careers. They had divorced when he was in the first grade. Both had remarried, and his mother had had a few "live-ins" along the way. He seemed not to belong in either family, and had the sense that he was essentially disposable, though nothing overt was ever said. His parents had provided him with lots of stuff—he never lacked the "in things." There weren't any guidelines at home, except a general "don't get into trouble" admonition now and then. Nothing in his life or thinking connected him with anything else. At least his parents and stepparents were somewhat intelligent and successful professionals. That gave him some incentive to achieve.

Basically, he grew up hanging out with school friends, watching the tube, and going to whatever was called home to eat and sleep (most of the time). He had explored all of the fads and trendy stuff, as well as dabbled in escapes from boredom (drugs, sexual experimentation, New Age come-ons). When he got tired of all those dead ends he resorted to his computer, the Web, virtual reality, and the fantasy world of cyberspace. Academic stuff had never been much of a hurdle. He sort of backed into the field of environmental engineering simply because he had this lurking sense that it was an area overlooked by most of the American consumer society.

But once out of school, established in a well-paying position, and on his own, the *big questions* began to close in on Chip and evoke in him the sense that something larger than life was missing. He had roamed the bookstores and sampled the religion and self-help sections. It was all there: Oriental religions, satanism, New Age, Mother Earth, psychological and physical culture stuff. "Nothing," as he said, "stirred my cocoa."

"It was like my path led me up to a big smooth wall and came to a dead end. I hoped there would be a door in it, or through it, somewhere. How could you find it? Was it a formula? A secret? A combination of things: something you pushed, or said? But all I got was silence! A big question got even bigger: Is there anything out there, any meaning, any hope? What is life all about? Does anybody care? How do you sort through all the hype and phoniness and broken trusts? How do you sort through the deceptions? Who could I take seriously? Only more darkness, and no answers. Most of my friends are as screwed up as I am. I mean, like, it's not hard to figure out the drug route. If life is meaningless and boring and hopeless, why not? It never appealed to me, but it does to a lot of my friends.

"Look, insofar as the guys' magazines are concerned, I'm a success. Face it, I've got a pretty healthy and sexy bod—you know, tight abs, and all of that. I've got a good, well-paying job. I've got more stuff than I can use and a comfortable loft. I can take trips, go skiing, have nice holidays. Hey! It's not hard to entertain yourself to death. But it's all so innocuous. I keep feeling along that big wall, looking for some clue, some hidden door.

"It was only sort of a momentary thing that made me look into that church this morning. I mean, I've never even been in a church building. Why should I bother? I walk past that one several times a week, but it was just one more big impersonal building that looked old and musty. I have wondered what it was all about but never lingered on the question. If Kate hadn't been there, I would probably have just written it off as a weird cult that some folks like, and a waste of a good Sunday morning. But then, hey! I've only had that one brief experience of it. So who am I to judge?

"But, like, something in my life really is missing *big time*. So, is following Jesus primarily about going to those productions at some church building? Or is there somewhere that you go to get into the stuff that really counts?"

Jong

Jong picked it up: "My experience is almost exactly the opposite of yours, Chip. Christianity came to Korea over a century ago, and its missionaries presented a very structured and disciplined version of the faith. It took root and fit perfectly with our Confucian culture's work ethic, respect for family, and all that. My people believed in Jesus, and accepted and studied the Bible as God's written Word to us. What developed were very strong Christian family structures and a highly disciplined church life. My problem as a second generation Korean-American is trying to relate the Christian faith that my parents brought to this country with the permeating secularism of North America. Here the church lacks much structure and discipline, not to mention a clearly understood faith.

"It is so altogether different from my heritage out of Korea. Not only that, but because so many of our churches here still hold services in Korean, it is increasingly difficult for my English-speaking generation to relate. Still, there is something strong and compelling about Korean Christianity that I miss here. So, I struggle with two diverse cultures. Add to that the struggle with the realities of the technological and scientific world in which I have lived these past ten years. Somehow it has consuming worldviews that are often alien to my own belief in one Creator-God. We'll pursue that if you want."

Barbara

Then it was Barbara's turn. She grew up in a very strict, almost legalistic African-American tradition that didn't have much room for her adolescent testing of the boundaries. "I mean, like, we went to church, 'did church,' all the time—it seemed like every day of the week. I wanted to hang out with my friends, do what they did, and all that. My parents and the preachers were always on my case, warning me that Satan was after me—he probably was—and that people who lived like I wanted to were going to hell. You know, all that hellfire and damnation stuff. I lived always with the fear that God was right on my back trying to catch me doing or thinking something ever so slightly wrong so he could zap me. But, even with that, my family was wonderful. Loved me. Gave me structure and stability. But you know how teenage kids are—I wanted freedom, whatever that was.

"So I went to college and got my freedom, and hung up all of that Christian stuff for a while. Tried everything, like *everything*. You know what I mean? You know what? A real bummer. It was crazy. No direction. Would you believe I even began to miss church? I used to snicker at those preachers up there whoopin' and putting on a show. But down in my insides, there was something there that I longed for. So I began to find my way back like a prodigal daughter. In law school I linked up with some Christian kids who were trying to fit their faith into what law school offered.

"I got out of law school and went to work in the legal department of our company. I found that I wasn't alone. There were quite a few people around who were followers of Jesus. They didn't make a big deal of it, but it became obvious in quiet ways. That's where I met Jong. We started going to a Christian business persons' luncheon at a church up the street from our office building. Every week they would bring in someone significant in the business and professional community to share his or her successes and failures in implementing faith in the workplace. It was really good. Those luncheons put us in touch with other neat Christian folks. Face it, there are a lot of stresses when you try to live out your Christian faith in the workplace. I should know. Hey—I'm a lawyer! Lawsuits everywhere. Legal ethics—is that an oxymoron or what?

"The church thing is still up in the air. Most of my Christian friends from this neighborhood and from work go to churches here in Midtown that are mostly white. I have this lover's quarrel with the church, and bounce between a church that Jong and I go to, and my family's church across town. Anyway, that's where I am."

Kate

A bit older than the others, Kate had taught English literature at a local university for some years. In continual contact with inquiring minds, she had developed a wonderful sense of humor, a penchant for being patient with obtuse students, and a sensitivity to real questions beneath the surface.

"I'm a product of an even different set of dynamics in my Christian faith. I grew up in a proper middle-class home where the church was part of the social ethos. But it was very nominal. It really didn't affect our family life much at all. Christmas and Easter stuff. But it was always there on the fringe of my mind. In high school I fell in with a bunch of kids in a Christian organization called Young Life, which was worlds of fun. I liked the leaders and the kids. After all kinds of crazy, high-energy activities we would sit around while the staff person teased us with the Christian message. That's the only way I can describe it. She hung the questions out there, and made us think, but in such an almost irreligious way that it took you off guard. It was in that context that I began to think seriously about Jesus, and ultimately decided that I wanted to follow him.

"I guess working on my degrees in English literature made me realize how profoundly our Western culture is influenced by the Christian faith and the Christian church. I mean, if you're not in touch with the biblical material, you miss a lot of the references.

"Then I became more and more enamored of, and amazed by, the diversity and place of the church in history and in different societies. Look back over the centuries in Russia, Europe, India, Great Britain—it's absolutely awesome. And I don't mean just one part of the church, like the Episcopalian—I mean Orthodox, Catholic, Protestant, Coptic, not to mention the ethnic diversity within those branches. Anyhow, I landed in the Episcopal Church simply because it has deep roots back into all of this Christian tradition—and I need roots. That much for starters. Oh, I have a lover's quarrel too. There is so much in the church that is embarrassing. But when I look at the bigger picture, I'll live with it because I can't live without it."

Confession Time

A thoughtful silence hung in the air. Finally Chip spoke. "OK. So maybe this is all great for you guys. It still doesn't make sense to me—at least not all of it. What does something that happened a couple of thousand years ago have anything to do with me and the rest of us in the twenty-first century? I mean, like, Jesus was an ancient. I'm a modern, probably a postmodern—whatever that means. That's one problem. Next question. So people get into religion. A lot of my friends get into religion. They practice meditation, or do the Gaia thing. Some are Jewish, some Islamic. Who's to say that they are not all as much into their religion as you are, and that it's not as meaningful as yours? Is that an OK question?

"I appreciate the fact that you're trying to make sense to me, but you're not. You don't sound like you're even talking about the same experience. You guys are coming from different places and using different concepts to explain why you're into Jesus. Am I right? I mean, it's like when my printer glitches and I click the print command and all I get is this garbled bunch of symbols with an occasional word I recognize. That's about how I am with this conversation. I've got to make out what the connection is between what's missing in me and all the stuff you're talking about, and then factor in all these other unanswered questions."

Kate assured him that if the questions were on his mind, they were necessary. But she also wanted to know what other contradictions he was referring to earlier in the day. Chip's response was to turn the question on them. "You all sound as though it is so easy and that you didn't have any trouble buying into the Christian thing. Didn't you, or don't you have trouble with things not fitting? Any doubts about it? When you look at it objectively, does it all make sense to you? I looked around at those people in that church this morning and they looked like they were either 'zoned' or on cruise control, or were bored silly—totally passive while supposedly into something so awesome as God. Come on!"

"Look at it this way, Chip," Barbara interrupted. "You're talking here about a community of belief. It's part of a story that goes back probably four thousand years or so. But about two thousand years ago the really big event took place, and that was when Jesus landed on the scene of human history and made the astounding claim that to see him was to see God the Father and Creator. Such a claim was so preposterous that it blew some of them away. But there was so much evidence that he was telling the truth that the folk whom he called to be with him became the first generation of Christians, the first church. They based their new lives on what Jesus taught them, on what he did, but most of all on the fact that he had foretold his death by execution and that he would rise from the dead—and he did! That's mind-boggling enough. So for all of these centuries there has been one generation of Christian folk after another who have carried on that community. But, face it, Chip: People forget, they get it mixed up, they do get bored with it, they wander off into stupid stuff—and you get contradictions. It happens. So if you see contradictions, and screwed-up interpretations of the Christian faith, welcome to the club. So do we!"

"I'm turned off by so much consumer culture Christianity," Kate chimed in. "I have enough sense of the integrity of the Christian message to see that too many of its highly visible spokespersons today alter it to make it marketable to the fickle masses. I'm not questioning their sincerity, but it still offends me. Then I look at church history and am reminded that the lights have gone out in the Christian community time and again, in every generation. But at the same time they have gone *out* in one place, they have gone *on* somewhere else, where no one would ever have expected. In every generation there have been those in the church who have dealt profoundly with the real questions of life. What is even more awesome is the good stuff that has happened when people live out their faith in Jesus—life and meaning and blessing seem to follow in their wake.

"Chip, my *turn-off* with the Christian faith is with those who reduce it to something so banal that they never get to 'the stuff that really counts,' as you put it a little while ago. My *turn-on* is that it answers my questions about what my life and all of this creation are about. That might be a piece of your empty spot, Chip—both personally and as an environmentally aware guy."

"Yeah, I've been troubled by some of the stuff in the Christian picture," Barbara offered. "But there were two positive things that got my attention. One was when I realized from the teachings of Jesus and his followers that God's love and forgiveness of messed-up people like me was overwhelming and all-consuming. That was demonstrated in what Jesus did. The other thing was when I saw and heard the Christian emphasis on justice, on God's design for human society, on freedom. For me, as an African-American, that was really, really good news, and it had been focally significant in my tradition from slave days. So you take the good news with the bad and put them in perspective."

"Well, looks like I opened a can of worms!" said Chip with a grin. "I'm not alone in having some hang-ups. Your turn, Jong."

"I think I've hinted at my turn-offs before, and it comes from my own Korean-Christian tradition confronting American culture. I'm turned off by the superficiality of so much of the Christian presence that doesn't change people or communities—and with no accountability. I find much American Christianity fairly mind-less, and far too individualistic. It is so much 'What can God do for me?' stuff. I don't think you can approach Jesus Christ with that kind of privatistic and subjective selfishness. What continues to attract me is that I find so many Christians who are good scholars and more intellectually honest than those who are not Christians. I know that may sound a bit elitist, but it's true. That for me, as a scientist, is a plus. There are questions behind the questions that my secular counterparts seem unwilling to face up to. But again, Chip, I cannot deny my own heritage, and that also is part of what persuades me about the reality of Christian faith. I have experienced the strength and order that comes from a community of Christian faith, the life of prayer that is effective. So I too have to weigh the contradictions and make choices."

Chip reflected on all of this. "I guess that if I'm honest there are some things on the fringes of my mind that have made me a bit curious. Like that little old Christian lady in India who checked out a while back [Mother Teresa], or that whole thing in Westminster Abbey when Princess Diana died. That was heavy, deep, moving, though I didn't understand a whole lot of what it meant. It obviously meant a lot to all of those people weeping and singing. It got me thinking that maybe somebody had found the door. But it's like another world to me."

The poignant moment came at the very end of the evening, when Chip let down his guard for a moment and became very vulnerable: "Thanks for tonight. I'm still confused, and in a good sense you guys have confused me even more by telling me your own stories. But something is still blank in me. Then again, I've heard something from your hearts. Tell me something: If I walk this path with you, and get serious abut Jesus, will you guys walk with me and pour your lives into mine?" Without explaining what he meant, he took his jacket, said good night, and left the trio standing there.

WHERE TO GO FROM HERE _____

This story is based on true composite conversations. In an introductory way, it portrays the task before us. It is the Chips of this world who call forth what follows. What are we to do with this

Subversive Jesus, Radical Grace

vast spiritual hungering all around us, hiding behind facades of indifference and sullenness? And what are we to do with a church so preoccupied with lesser things, and so ill-equipped to be God's agent of hope and good news? We Christians need to be persuaded that the message of Jesus Christ is still the Bread of Life so that when men and women "taste" him they never hunger anymore. Yet somehow that message has been so enculturated, so reduced and trivialized, that it is hidden from many people floundering in hopelessness.

Every day we are surrounded by both acquaintances and strangers who are the real people whom Jesus came "to seek and to save." How are we to perceive our place as bearers of good news and hope? The conversation between Chip and the three Christian friends raises and leaves with us haunting and insistent questions:

- How are we to be Christ's witnesses among secular acquaintances who are biblically illiterate, without moral absolutes, for whom "truth" is thought to be defined by and for each individual in his or her own circumstances, and who are oblivious to the church?
- What darkness, what unanswered questions, what loneliness goes on behind the healthy and successful exteriors of our smiling colleagues? Or, what lies behind the despair and hopelessness (even nihilism) of so many urban youth, both from upper-class suburbs as well as from scenes of urban blight?
- What spiritual hungering is hidden in their "bored self-sufficiency"?
- How has our own gospel been effectively hidden from these by the very church called to embody God's Word of hope and love?
- How are we (the Kates, Barbaras, and Jongs of the Christian community) to be equipped and fashioned to be the agents of God's compassionate love to those outside (such as Chip) who long to find the door that will lead them out of darkness and into their heart's true home?

▸ What do we need to understand about God's purpose in Christ and about our calling into that purpose to get us beyond the contradictions, reductions, and misunderstandings that hide the good news of God, or cause to stumble those whom Jesus came to seek and to save?

▸ What will it take to make us contagiously Christian in an increasingly difficult—if not downright resistant—North American culture?

That's the task before us. How do we find God's design in such a quest?

Before we proceed, one of Chip's observed contradictions needs to be acknowledged. There is a price to pay for the Christian faith. God's gospel does, in fact, bring those who follow Jesus into a life that is unimaginably blessed and new and empowered and free, full of hope and meaning. But the plausibility structures of our present human community do not respond positively to the teachings of Jesus, simply because he testifies that its works are evil.[1] There are demands of the gospel that need to be laid on the table along with the promises. In short, to follow Jesus is like acquiring the greatest treasure there is, but "if anyone would come after me, he must deny himself and take up his cross and follow me."[2] This is the uncomfortable piece of the gospel that we dare not trivialize.

SOME DETERMINING PRINCIPLES

1. We need to look seriously at how Jesus and his message totally *redefine* life and its meaning (not to mention many words and concepts, such as power, joy, hope, comfort, blessedness, to name only a few).

2. We need to accept our calling to be God's mission-minded community; to not argue, but to be an alternative people; to live and articulate who God is, who we are, what God has done in Christ, and how following him makes us new.

Subversive Jesus, Radical Grace

3. We need to be free to realize that for every generation and for every culture and subculture, the evangelistic task will take on different approaches and be nuanced to speak to the context and hungerings of each. Still the message will maintain its basic New Testament integrity. The New Testament itself demonstrates this very principle in its many approaches that bring us to one Lord, Jesus Christ.

That all begins with *God*, who is our Good News!

CHAPTER TWO

You Begin with God

*I've got a problem. I haven't got a clue what you guys
are talking about when you talk about God. I mean,
like, how would anybody really know God, understand
what God is all about? Come on! Any God that I could
figure out wouldn't be worth the effort. And if I designed
my own God, I'd be sure to screw that up, too, and
leave something out.*

—Chip

Though we need never be apologetic about the fact that we
believe that God *is*, and that he is the "heart's true home," we
must remember to throttle back and look and listen very carefully at
the common denominators shared by Chip and his generation of
twenty-first-century adults. These young men and women, whether
successful professionals or floating and hopeless street kids, live by
their own wits. Many of them are cut off from social and historical
structures that the rest of us who are older may take for granted.

Listening to Chip's three friends in their conversation also
makes us realize that the task before us has many dimensions, and
that no small definition of the evangelistic mandate will suffice.
Awakenings to faith, or aroused spiritual hungerings, come in many
forms and by many avenues. But they have one goal in common,
though it may be totally unknown or unformed in those being

awakened. That one goal is God! The haunting sense of lostness, or the despairing sense of incompleteness (or hopelessness) that Chip articulated, is a lostness from God; it is the creature longing for the Creator. We must, then, begin at the beginning. After all, *evangelism* is about God!

GOD? SAY WHAT?

So right away we have a problem. To this neo-pagan (to put it charitably) generation which has formed Chip, the very word *God* is a totally confusing non-concept. For us to simply engage in "God talk," as though that were somehow serving the cause, is a no-brainer. To say that "God loves you and has a wonderful plan for your life" assumes they know about God and can relate to the sincerity of love! Multiple distortions, caricatures, and images of God floating around in the cultural ethos only exacerbate the problem. Think for a moment of Chip's struggle with the idea of God as "merciful Father" when the absentee fathers whom he has experienced have been such a question mark for him. He stands before us as the flesh-and-blood evidence of the groundless assumption among many well-meaning Christian folk that everybody understands who God is. That assumption is even questionable inside the church. At best, people have some awareness of "the Force" (as in *Star Wars*) or the "Higher Power" (as in most Twelve-Step programs).

Put yourself in Chip's shoes. He has stumbled into a new set of friends who have a whole different set of faith assumptions and are experiencing a community of this shared faith, all of which are outside the scope of his comprehension. This is a totally unique (even disorienting) experience for him. These friends have a center, some concept of something or someone called *God*, that catches his attention but for the present eludes him.

And as if this were not enough, we need to factor in the way that language is popularly manipulated and deconstructed. There is a prevailing cynicism about *words* in general. *God*, then, is simply one more *nothing-word*.

So how do we proceed?

For one, we need to learn to *listen* very carefully. We should learn that lesson from the God whom we worship. God is always tuned in to the questions that reflect the confusion and lostness of the persons whom he has created. More specifically, look at and learn from Jesus. Those *outside* of the family of faith are the ones we want to bring *inside.* Jesus came to seek and rescue those who were *out there* in their lostness. And we only have to read the accounts of Jesus' ministry and realize how he listened intently and sensitively to people like the woman at the well, the first disciples, Zaccheus, Mary and Martha, the rich young ruler, and Nicodemus. He heard their inner longings, questions, and confusions. He knew that they were created by and for God, and that God was their "heart's true home." But he listened to the questions, spoken and unspoken, that expressed this quest before responding to their need, such as:

▶ Who am I?
▶ What am I doing here?
▶ What does my life mean?
▶ Where did I come from?
▶ Does anybody care that I'm here?
▶ Does anybody love me? Accept me for who I am?
▶ Is there anything beyond death? Or any hope in this life?
▶ Is there any structure to which I am accountable?
▶ What is the ultimate in human fulfillment? "What is the chief and highest end of man?"[1]

There is an obvious sense in which Chip was alluding to these unanswered questions in telling the others of his emptiness and his quest for a *door.* But it is also true that the others told him of questions that had brought them to faith in Jesus Christ. When Jong told of his journey, there was the question of: How do we know? Is there truth? This is the *epistemological* question. Barbara had a question about human behavior, about social justice, to which she found an answer: How do we know what is right and wrong? How do we behave? This is the *ethical* question. Kate, in a different way, had pursued the questions about reality, about life and its mystery and meaning. These are the *metaphysical* questions. For these three, their questions led them ultimately to Jesus Christ. Chip voiced a major question of his own generational culture: Is there any *hope?*

The daughters and sons of God listen very carefully to the questions, to the hearts, of those still outside of the family of God's love. Oddly enough, such questions often come in the lyrics of popular songs, or in the seemingly mindless dialogue of television sitcoms!

THE ASSUMPTIONS BEFORE THE FACT

Even before we tackle the mystery of God, we need to acknowledge that we begin with an assumption that God *is!* Everyone begins with some before-the-fact assumptions (whether or not he or she knows it) that need to be identified. Some persons are *theists*, some are *deists*, or *atheists*, or *agnostics*, or *secular humanists*, not to mention those who are formed by all kinds of other religious and philosophical constructs. To put it baldly, each of these positions is a *faith position*. Each is based on some (articulate or inarticulate) assumption about reality, which is not at all provable by any rationalistic or scientific method. These are, if you will, pre-theoretical, or presuppositional faith assumptions.

For instance, I have a longtime friend, a very gifted scientist, who simply rejects the notion of a God. He and I, within the context of our friendship, have had different faith assumptions for years. He says that there is simply "nothing out there." In his view, we're quite on our own. One point that I can never quite get across to him in our conversations is that his no-god, nothing-out-there position is as much an act of faith (and maybe more so) as my position that there is one God who is the Creator and Savior of humankind. He doesn't buy that. From my faith assumption, his faith assumption leaves him out there on what someone described as "the bottomless, boundless sea of chance."

Agnosticism (that we can't or don't know) is as much a faith assumption as is a trust-belief that we can know God. *Secular humanism* (that humankind's welfare in the present life is to be determined without reference to belief in God or the future state) is a position of faith that is there before reason ever kicks in. The other *world religions* are obviously faith positions as are the popular "religions" closer to home in North American mass culture— *consumerism:* true life is in buying more things; *materialism:* true life is in owning things; *hedonism:* life is only meaningful in seeking pleasure; or *cynicism:* "Who cares?"

More distressing are the folk who are so brain-dead and psychically numb that they appear to have no response to anything. All such persons are part of our picture. The point here is that when we Christian folk introduce God into the human equation, we are only being quite honest about that which is our pre-theoretical beginning place: "Before the fact, here's where I begin to consider life and reality and meaning. Here are my faith assumptions. What are yours?"

THE MYSTERY OF GOD THE CREATOR

First, honesty. To Chip's challenge about "How can anybody really know God?" we can only respond: "Good question! And you are correct: God is in a very real sense *unknowable.*" God is beyond our human categories. We who are the creatures can hardly begin to comprehend the Creator. It's like expecting a computer to comprehend the computer scientist who developed it, or like expecting the light bulb to comprehend Edison. There is mystery here. How much of the infinite can our very finite intellectual facilities take in? The church has used such terms as transcendent, unknowable, incomprehensible, infinite, and eternal to convey the awesome otherness of the God whom we believe and worship. The mystery of God is always before us. There is always that dimension of holy agnosticism which we accept, and which generates true humility on our part.

And if God had not purposed to *reveal* himself, if he had hidden himself in his transcendence or remained silent, we would face an impossible task in attempting to try to know him. The beginning of God's goodness is that this "beyond knowing" God has also designed us so that we, as persons, can know all that we need to know about him as a personal God, worship and enjoy Him, and be in harmony with all of creation. That is to say, happily, that God has not left us in the dark about who he is and what is his purpose. It is upon the basis of that *revelation* of God that we proceed.

The God Who Designs to Be Known: Creation

One of the ironies of Chip's generation is that they are much more environmentally aware than most previous generations. They see the delicate balance of nature. They are alarmed by global warming. They observe the fragile ecological systems. One would think that such awareness would point them to an "intelligent design" and to the Designer-Creator responsible for such handiwork. For the biblical writers it did exactly that: "The heavens declare the glory of God; the skies proclaim the work of his hands."[2] Or another writer notes: "What may be known about God is plain . . . because God has made it plain to them. For since the creation of the world God's invisible qualities—his eternal power and divine nature—have been clearly seen, being understood from what has been made."[3] And though the eyes of our friends may not, for the present, see or understand this, it is there all the same. The goodness and wonder of God are *seen* in everything he has made.

Just look at our own bodies, replete with musculature, dexterity, the awesome instrument called the brain, sexuality and the reproductive system, digestion, senses such as sight, hearing, smell, taste, and touch, capacities of reflection and imagination . . . all point to an Intelligent Designer.

Nature is a double "Wow!" The more we discover, the more we explore, the more we know, the more fascinating and incredible it becomes. Our God is an artist, a craftsman of infinite creative ability. The beauty, the harmony, the seasons, the sights and smells and diversity . . . all reveal so much of the character and nature of God. It's not a bad place to initiate some conversations with the X and Y generations!

The God Who Designs to Be Known: The Narrative of God's Goodness

If God is a non-concept to many of our acquaintances, then the story of God's self-revelation in the Bible may be even more of a dark hole for them.[4] This book (or set of books) consists of sixty-six documents, deeply rooted in history, which tell of the Creator God revealing his design and demonstrating his heart. It speaks of God interacting both severely and mercifully with a somewhat obstinate and rebellious humankind—always inviting them into a dynamic and personal (as well as societal/national) relationship with himself!

In broad strokes the biblical narrative reveals God, and the extent to which he will go to be known by his creation. It reveals an agenda, a mission if you will, which demonstrates the heart of God. It grows on you. God becomes larger and more wonderfully good as you see him coming again and again, revealing, communicating, and demonstrating his agenda to give us a new song in our hearts.

When we engage our friends *outside*, the Chips of our acquaintance, we must be quite candid that our faith assumptions are deeply rooted in our acceptance that God has revealed himself in history, and that the biblical narratives are a faithful communication of that revelation of God to us. This is just who and what we are! We didn't make this all up, or invent God. But such confidence is an assumption that we share. This concept of "God-making-himself-known" is so much a display of God's goodness.

Our lives in the faith community of the twenty-first century are part of the story of God's goodness that dates back several millennia. We find our roots in a narrative of God's self-revelation that has existed from the mists of prehistory. That self-revelation comes to a sharp focus in a most awesome and unimaginable demonstration of God's goodness—the *Incarnation*—in which God came into human history and lived for a while among us in the person of Jesus of Nazareth.

It is important for us to be storytellers, to be able to walk with our friends back into this narrative. In the story told in chapter one, Kate recalled references to Scripture and theology replete in the writings of her favorite literary figures. Tragically, many of the present younger generation would miss those references altogether, and so miss some of the depth and beauty of this same literature. So be aware that our biblical story is not something we can *assume* with our conversation partners.

The biblical author Mark, for instance, speaks of "the good news of God."[5] The Chips of this world would naturally be expected to ask: "God? Who in the world is God? What is this God like whose news is good and is being reported?" They have been deceived by too many hokey advertisements and religious charlatans. In a culture that affirms multireligious pluralism, they want to know: "Who is God? Is God good news? How can you make a claim that your God is the one true God? Show me the good news! Don't just talk!"

BACK TO THE BEGINNING

To answer the questions Who am I? and Where did I come from?, we must begin at the beginning. That's exactly what our communal, or biblical, narrative does: "In the beginning God."[6] In the primordial mists of a formless cosmic void is God the Creator. Within the space of a few short chapters this biblical account is wonderfully enlightening. God the Creator progressively brought into being order and form and beauty out of nothingness.[7] At every stage of the process, the magnificent Creator stopped, looked upon his handiwork, and declared: "It is good!" God our Creator is an artist: beauty, color, harmony, rhythms, complementarity.

Then, amazingly, and more to the point of who we are, he created, as the crown of his design, a man and a woman "in his own image." He created humankind with all manner of capacities that the other creatures did not possess. Primarily, God created the man and the woman as living spirits (not robots or automatons) who could commune in intimacy with him, with the transcendent Creator. Isn't that amazing? He made them to be caretakers of his creation. Everything created was in wholesome *Shalom*,[8] in perfect and fulfilling harmony. The plants and animals and all that God had made were absolutely what they were designed to be. They lived together in unity with each other and the Creator. Consider also the reality that

God made the man and woman as distinctly different yet complementary physical beings, male and female. God said, "It is not good for the man to be alone," and thus was the creation of the most intimate of human relationships. The beginning of oneness, caring, procreation, and sexuality (that mysterious, powerful, hormonal, physical, and emotional expression of creative intimacy) is found here. God created family as the first nurturing, supportive human community. God is good.

VIRUS IN THE SYSTEM

This chapter is about God. But then again, we are speaking of God in the context of the cultural *chaos*, which is the result of a violation of the good—the *Shalom*—that was his intended purpose. We are speaking of God as *Light* in the context of darkness. So we need to make a short side trip at this point. The violation of the *Shalom* was like a virus inserted into a computer program; it was the original and ultimate screwup. Death and darkness entered the scene and the design was profaned. But it is with this as the context that God shows us his heart!

The violation is presented in a brief episode at the beginning of the Bible and it explains worlds about the conduct of humankind ever since (we'll come back to this in more detail in the next chapter, but we need to introduce it now). The story tells of an intrusion of something quite alien, of an attempt by the creature to contrive a life and reality on its own terms, which totally missed the point of the Creator. It was an attempt to live without reference to the mind and will and being of the Creator in whom and for whom it all existed and upon whom it was all-dependent. The tragic lesson here is that (like all humankind since who have missed the point of God) Adam and Eve remind us of a two-year-old asserting: "I can do it by myself!" Or a petulant teenager saying: "I don't need your help." These two primordial parents sought to make God the fall guy for their disobedience and foibles. It is a classical Freudian passing of the buck. Adam protests: "The woman whom you gave me, she made me do it!" In other words, "It's all your fault." So God has become the fall guy for human rebellion for all of Adam and Eve's progeny. To this day people assert that they can accept a God who meets their criteria of acceptance, but not that "angry and vindictive God of the Old Testament."

But quite the opposite is true. Look again! The sheer and unimaginable goodness of God shines forth in the narrative of the Old Testament. These documents demonstrate time and again, and magnificently, the patient goodness of God, and God does it right in the teeth of this primordial betrayal and rebellion by his own foolish creatures. God comes to them, calls them by name, and asks the original *evangelistic question:* "Where are you now?" The infinitely good Creator calls upon them to confess how tragically they had missed the point of it all. Then he reviews some of the inevitable consequences of their violation of his *Shalom.* But God also lets it be known that their betrayal has not taken him by surprise.

What unfolds, rather, is God's unmistakable agenda. He is jealous for his creation's total and ultimate well-being, its *Shalom.* Thus right in the face of this rebellion, this *virus,* God made known that in his good purpose he had a plan, a "deeper magic" as C. S. Lewis defines it.[9]

He declared that some future and as yet unseen "seed of a woman"[10] would be the instrument of an ultimate deliverance of humankind from the throes of the evil enchantment into which they have now entered. And somehow, in the mystery of it all, God would deal a mortal stroke to the perpetrator of this rebellion, the *serpent!*[11]

God does not abandon his own at all. Grace begins to show its first sprouts here. Craig Barnes defines *grace* as "whatever it takes for God to come and get us."[12] It is just such a merciful, gracious, purposeful, passionate God who begins to demonstrate his goodness and his everlasting love right from the beginning. Is this *good news* or what?

The God Who Designs to Be Known: A People Called Israel

The goodness of God toward the whole world emerges quite early in the biblical story. In the Middle East there dwelled a Semite by the name of Abram. He was (however you explain it) a God-fearer, someone who believed in the one true God. God had his attention. As Abram (who later was renamed Abraham) responded to God's communication and showed his commitment to God, he received the promise that in his seed, his progeny, "all the people-groups of the earth would be blessed."

Once again, don't miss the missionary agenda of God. God designs to bless all the people of the earth. That word *bless* is loaded! Everything is to be brought into perfect harmony with the Creator.

The story of the family of Abraham actually occupies the rest of the biblical narrative. Abraham's grandson Jacob was a colorful, volatile, and dubious personality, who in a transforming encounter with God was renamed Israel, the name that identifies the Jewish people to this day. Move down the corridor of history several centuries and these progeny of Abraham, now two million-plus strong, had become slaves in Egypt. They were miraculously delivered out of this powerful empire's grip under the leadership of Moses, another of those pivotal personalities who was responsive to God. It was to him that God revealed his special name: YHWH (or Yahweh).

THE GOODNESS OF GOD IN THE LAW OF GOD_____

Next on God's agenda was the historic moment when he constituted Israel as a nation at the foot of Mount Sinai (Horeb). What is fascinating, given the promise spoken to Abraham hundreds of years earlier, is that Israel is now called to be "a kingdom of priests and a holy nation."[13] In other words they were to demonstrate before the world a different kind of humanity. They were to be wonderfully related to God, and in sync with God's purpose for all creation. But this reality was dependent upon their obeying God fully and keeping the covenant he was making with them.

This covenant and the instructions God included (the Torah) in that dramatic encounter are more than a blueprint for their life together. They tell us about what makes life to be what God intended it to be, both as individuals and a community. Far from being restrictive and stifling, these instructions are the key to *Shalom,* to God's harmonious design. It is not incidental that he quite candidly lets them know that as they walk within this design, this law, they would experience all kinds of good things—blessings! Conversely, when and if they ignored or violated it (which they ultimately did), they could expect the pain and consequences of their disobedience. Even these judgments reveal the goodness of God. Why should God not take seriously that which would be destructive of *Shalom?* The creation of God functions harmoniously only when it is in sync with the mind and purpose of the Creator. It all fits!

In the Ten Commandments (also called the Decalogue) God speaks of his good purpose for his people. These simple operating principles speak volumes about what creates true *blessedness,* and makes Israel *holy.* Look at each one in my own loose paraphrase of God addressing the children whom he loves:

1. It is my ultimate *good news* for you that you learn that I really am the one and only God who loves you, who made it all, and who called you to be my own. Take note, then, that any *god* invented by your human ingenuity is folly, and simply doesn't make it. You are mine and I am jealous for your hearts and minds.

2. Oh yes, there will always be a human proclivity to reduce my reality as God the Creator to something more manageable by human wills, to make gods of things, to worship the creature more than the Creator. Don't do it! It won't work. The *good news* for you is that you have me, and I am the one who brings you into your true purpose. Anything else is a disaster.

3. The *good news* for you is that, in your relationship of integrity with me, you don't use my name to cloak your own duplicity, or try to hide behind my name when you are up to no good. My name is who I Am, and I don't take my character lightly, nor should you. I bless you when you faithfully live out the calling to be mine. Your relationship to me is a privilege and not to be manipulated. Don't forget it!

4. The *good news* for you is that I want you (and you need) to have a regular rhythm of work and worship in which I am your model. Your work will take on meaning as you reflect on who I am, and what I am working out in your lives, and in your community, and in the world. So I am giving you a day of rest, a Sabbath. One day in seven, just to stop what you are doing, and focus on me and your relationship to me. Not only so, but when you have worked well for six days, you need physical rest. Both work and worship are part of my design. When you neglect either one, it all begins to unravel. This means not only you, but also those for whom you are responsible (employees and the like). Remember, I labored in creation for six days, and then stopped to reflect on it. You can do no less!

5. The *good news* for you is that there is a purposeful order in the human community. There are those who are given responsibility in nurture, provision, protection, caring, and authority. Then there are those who are dependent, who need care and protection and provision, and who are responsible to those in authority. This begins in the human family and in the place I have given to mothers and fathers. It extends into the larger human family and community. This order is to be honored. When it is violated, anarchy, suffering, and destruction follow in its wake.

6. The *good news* for you is that human life is my creation and is most sacred. Never demean, destroy, or dehumanize the sanctity of life. You must do everything within your power to provide for human life so that it is not destroyed by homicide, indifference, or passive neglect.

7. The *good news* for you is that I created you as male and female, two wonderfully distinct and complementary sexes. I did this for the purpose of true intimacy within

the sanctity of marriage. Marriage is my creation. That sexual relation between husband and wife is sanctified. True intimacy is within the marriage bond and the marriage bed. Out of this comes the procreation of children, who also need the context of intimacy, nurture, permanence, and true love. As powerful and mysterious and volatile as sexuality is, its true expression is a gift and pleasure to be enjoyed by husbands and wives only.

8. The *good news* for you is the sanctity of property. Your caring for others involves also caring for what is rightfully theirs. There are boundaries that are good. In your love for others you will give them provisions and gifts, but it is not within my *Shalom* that you take by stealth or deceit or force that which is not yours, or deny any the means of human sustenance through inadequate wages or legal shenanigans.

9. The *good news* for you is the sanctity of truth-telling. I am the God of truth. My Word is faithful and true. Yours must be also. The goodness of life is experienced when you speak with integrity and truthfulness. Otherwise life is built on deceit, duplicity, and gossip, which is definitely bad news.

10. The *good news* for you is that I want you to be contented with life. Contentment with life's essentials is a huge blessing. Some will be in different places and have different stations and more or less possessions. But contentment is my gift to you. There is a good ambition that strives to accomplish honorable goals. That is to be commended. But dissatisfaction (and greed) that makes you resentful of the accomplishments and possessions of others is a disease that will eat you up. Simplicity of life is a gift of my goodness.

As God continued to explicate for Israel what made them unique and blessed, he went on to give all kinds of fascinating principles

Subversive Jesus, Radical Grace

having to do with environment, diet, community order, sanitation, and caring for all of the citizens, especially those helpless and without human resources for food and shelter, clothing and justice. These reveal such an insight into God's nature and caring, which is a key to understanding *Shalom*.

But it is also important to note that God was very aware that these folk would miss the point and screw up (to use Chip's term). So out of his goodness and mercy, God provided a way of being forgiven, of being reconciled to him and to each other. These dramatic sacrifices and the system of atonement became a central part of Israel's life.

DESCENT INTO CHAOS, THEN PROMISE_____

In broad strokes, this Old Testament narrative reveals the extent to which God would go to work out his design, even with a people who seemed intent on doing it all wrong! God purposed to be their only King, to guide them and protect them and relate to them. He wanted to be their Helper, to respond to their needs. He would rescue them from dangers and forgive their failures. But the narrative is also one of the dismal history of the *virus* of attempted autonomy at work. Even with this frightening record of disobedience, God revealed his nature of being patient and long-suffering and forgiving: "If my people, who are called by my name, will humble themselves and pray and seek my face and turn from their wicked ways, then I will hear from heaven and will forgive their sin and will heal their land."[14]

On the brink of entering the land which God had promised to give them, Moses had spelled out for Israel exactly how God would accomplish his plan to bless their nation and other nations through them.[15] They could never again, as a nation, plead ignorance. They were called to a decision, and at that dramatic moment, they chose God. But Moses had also let them know of the seductions and temptations the *virus* would produce among them, and the dismal choices they would make. What follows in the rest of the Old Testament is the frightening record of Moses' warnings becoming reality.

Try as they might, Israel could not "do it by themselves." They could not prosper and be blessed without God. They became more and more a kingdom not of priests, but a copy of the pagan nations around them. They were anything but a *holy* nation exhibiting God's agenda of blessing to the other nations. They missed the point of their calling, and of God's design, and of their own covenant. They basically left God out of their national equation.

The God Who Designs to Be Known: Always Some Who Responded

In this fascinating and tragic story of God seeking and his people forgetting, there were always those special ones who did, in fact, love and fear God. God continued to reveal himself to them. There were the Judges and unique God-fearers like Ruth who spoke and obeyed the Word of the Lord at key times. And there was one king (in a long history of unfaithful kings) who had a heart of integrity toward God: David. For all of David's obvious human passions, he was a worshiper whose heart belonged to God. From him came most of the great poetry and prayers of worship in the Old Testament. And to David, God made the enigmatic and provocative promise that his throne would last forever. This seemed so unlikely in the generations that followed David, but there is the promise nevertheless.

God's agenda—his mission of blessing—would not be wrecked by Israel's unbelief and unfaithfulness. God's sovereign good purpose continued to shine through at unexpected moments. But after David, the *virus* took over again and with it came a dismal decline into pettiness, corruption, and paganism overlaid with a superficial temple worship which gave lip service to God but violated the intent of his covenant.

The God Who Designs to Be Known: The Prophets

Around the eighth century B.C. there began to appear on the scene some colorful and eccentric spokespersons for God: prophets. They were unique agents of God's revelation. Their message was not complicated, though it was often couched in imaginative language and metaphors. God's agenda remained unchanged, but the prophets began to give it a new perspective. What unfolds is how awesomely and unbelievably beautiful is the agenda of God to take even this national tragedy and to ultimately bring it all back into perfect and even more splendid harmony with himself. It is a "beyond asking or imagining" kind of love.

The prophets' message verbalized the results of Israel's failure to live according to their own calling and covenant. It reminded Israel of what Moses had predicted on the east bank of the Jordan River[16] that was now coming true. Judgment was about to happen — the people would be destroyed or taken into exile. The surrounding nations would prevail, but only because Israel had been unfaithful in its relationship to God, in its social contract within itself, and in its role as a nation of priests. The judgment fell upon them primarily because of their failures to keep the second table of the law: the law of love toward neighbors. They exploited the poor and homeless, were dishonest and sexually profligate.[17]

The prophets also laid bare the inadequacy of religion. The Israelites had an abundance of religious rites, but they had forgotten their purpose. Their inner life was in shambles. In graphic language God spoke through the prophets to say that he was nauseated by their empty and superficial religion. The people had forgotten him — the beginning and ending of all things, in whom creation found its true *Shalom*.

This calamitous period of Israel's existence also reveals that God is not to be ignored, trifled with, or taken for granted. When his *Shalom* is violated, and the sin virus produces inhumanity and injustice and destruction and death, then God, the righteous and ultimate Judge, is sure to act. Moreover, every time someone in these Old Testament narratives met with God, or was in his presence, they were (to put it mildly) totally overwhelmed, "blown away," and quite naturally terrified. This was true of Abraham, Moses, Isaiah, and others. The prophet Isaiah said that to come face-to-face with such perfection, which exposes all that is false and disobedient, is a meeting and a message that "will bring sheer terror."[18]

I bring this up at this point because as the followers of Jesus contemplate the dimensions of his message, they must take into account an awesome God, whose very being and character must be taken seriously. God calls upon his people to identify with that holiness, with his sovereign design for blessing all creation.

The God Who Designs to Be Known: A New Covenant?

It is at this point that the first faint strains of the "Deeper Magic" began to be heard. God had an extravagant plan unfolding, and it had to do with a moment in human history—an event—that no one would have imagined or predicted. He was about to interrupt the spiritual sleep of a faithless people, as well as the life-as-usual behavior of the rest of the human community. The prophets began to make noises about a *New Covenant*, about a Servant of God, about an Anointed One (*Messiah*) who would come.

God would create a new kind of relationship with humanity in which his law, his Word, would be written in their very minds and in their hearts. He would give them a new heart and would put his own Spirit in them so that they would respond spontaneously and with joy to his agenda. They would all know God and become zealous about his purpose for creation.[19]

This word of hope came at the threshold of a crushing national disaster. God let his disobedient and unfaithful people know that though they had violated every provision of his calling and covenant, he had plans for them and "a future and a hope."[20] The day would come when their God would once more "exult over [them] with loud singing."[21] And more . . .

> *For the mountains may depart and the hills be removed, but my steadfast love shall not depart from you, and my covenant of peace shall not be removed, says the Lord, who has compassion on you.*[22]

The God Who Designs to Be Known:
The Anointed Servant

The question arises as to *how* in the world God intended to accomplish this New Covenant. How would God effect forgiveness and cleansing for such a wayward lot? What begins to emerge in Isaiah's prophetic ministry is the promise of a *Servant!* This Servant picture is both compelling and illusive. Listen:

> *Behold my Servant, whom I uphold, my chosen, in whom my soul delights; I have put my Spirit upon him, he will bring forth justice to the nations. . . . He will not fail or be discouraged till he has established justice in the earth; and the coastlands wait for his law.*[23]

But this Servant also becomes something more of a stranger to the human imagination.

> *And to whom has the arm of the Lord been revealed?. . . he had no form or comeliness that we should desire him. He was despised and rejected by men; a man of sorrows, and acquainted with grief; . . . he was despised, and we esteemed him not. Surely he has borne our griefs and carried our sorrows; yet we esteemed him stricken by God, and afflicted. But he was wounded for our transgressions, and he was bruised for our iniquities; upon him was the chastisement that made us whole, and with his stripes we are healed.*[24]

The Servant of God is a sin-bearer? A healer? A substitute for transgressors? What next? How is the everlasting love of God going to play itself out? But wait, there is more to this Servant. The Servant is anointed with a set of ministries to those very helpless and marginalized folk who were very special to God's heart:

> *The Spirit of the Sovereign LORD is upon me, because the LORD has anointed me to preach good news to the poor. He has sent me to bind up the brokenhearted, to proclaim freedom for*

*the captives and release from darkness for the prisoners, to pro-
claim the year of the LORD'S favor and the day of vengeance of
our God, to comfort all who mourn.*[25]

What is most awesomely unfolded here is that God's design is
sure, and that he is going to provide the Servant as his agent to deal
with the *virus,* and to create the new community of *Shalom* in all of
its profound and unimaginable dimensions. The character of this
Servant of God gives us again an insight into God's heart. God's
anointing of the Servant by his Spirit is critical for our understanding of the scope of Jesus and his gospel. It is not a one-dimensional
message that has only to do with the forgiveness for sin in some
vague and inarticulate way, oblivious to the agenda of God.

It includes the forgiving grace of the offended God, to be sure.
But it includes much, much more. All that is caused by humankind's
sin of missing the point—all of the tragic social, economic, systemic, and personal destructiveness—is encompassed in God's great
salvation. God's good news gets bigger and bigger as we reflect on
this account—and it staggers our imagination! It reaches fullness
in Jesus, who came announcing that he is the Anointed Servant, the
Messiah, come to create the true Israel and to bring God's people
back from their exile and into God's Dominion. Which brings us
to our next topic.

The God Who Designs to Be Known:
The Coming Dominion of God

Lest my readers think that I have gotten carried away and forgotten Chip and his confusion over the concept of God, not so. There
is a piece of God's design that needs to be made clear because it
hits us straight on at the opening of the New Testament documents.
It relates to the *Dominion (Kingdom) of God,* which is somehow at
the very core of God's missionary agenda, and is somehow the fulfillment of the aforementioned *New Covenant.* So we proceed.

In the centuries at the end of the Old Testament period—after
Israel's return from captivity—*synagogues* (the places of gathering)
became the primary locus for much of Jewish life. These meeting

Subversive Jesus, Radical Grace

places had developed during the exile. It was in the synagogues that the Jewish people gathered to read and discuss the Law and the Prophets. It was in the synagogues that the rabbis became the very colorful and influential figures in Judaism (and are to this day).

In these synagogues, and in the Jewish community, the *hope* took on form in the developing expectation known as the *malkuth shamaim*, which is Aramaic for something like "the coming reign of Yahweh." The *malkuth shamaim* looked toward the day when Israel's God was going to intervene, lead them out of their exile, and inaugurate his dominion.[26] In the New Testament, this would be the kingdom of God, or kingdom of heaven. Accompanying this expectation was the growing expectation of the Anointed One *(Messiah)* who would somehow establish David's throne forever.

Yahweh Who Brings Salvation

As we tell and retell this story of God's involvement with the particular people called Israel, we begin to see and understand the person of the God who designs to be known, and who has a name: *Yahweh.* God is the Creator-God. God is the God who makes humankind with the capacity to know him and to live in relationship with himself. God loves and cherishes and plans for his people. God is the God who, though transcendent, wills to live in the midst of his people. God is the altogether and infinitely righteous God who hates all that violates and defiles and misses the point of creation. God is the God of mercy and long-suffering patience. God is the God who is mysterious in his ways. God is also faithful. God is his people's refuge and strength. Wisdom and knowledge begin with God. God is the God in whose presence is fullness of joy and at whose right hand are pleasures forevermore. In these stories and accounts of God and Israel, of God in human history, we come to know God-as-God is, or God's glory. There is something both warm and intimate on one hand, and awesome and fearsome on the other. The whole earth is full of God's glory.

This is our *really* good news! God is good news!

But this is only the threshold. If the glory of God is seen and known awesomely and wonderfully demonstrated in these Old Testament stories, then when we read the first pages of the New Testament we come face-to-face with an event that beggars the imagination, not to mention the capacity of language. Even the angels reach for an adequate verbal means to make the announcement. At the coming of Jesus they declare, *"Glory in the highest!"* The God who comes in flesh and blood is the God of Abraham, Isaac, and Jacob. God who comes in Jesus is not a new invention. Rather, he is *Jesus* which means *Yahweh Who Brings* (or *Is*) *Salvation.* The same God with whom we have walked in the pages of the Old Testament, now comes in a whole other self-revelation, the "seed of Abraham" who will bring blessing to the world.

But I'm getting ahead of myself. A discussion of the God who, in Christ, reconciles the world to himself will have to wait until chapter four. For now, as we seek to faithfully communicate to Chip and his counterparts outside of the household of faith, the words of Craig Barnes are to the point:

> *To live with the sacred God of creation means that we conduct our lives with a God who does not explain himself to us. It means that we worship a God who is often mysterious—too mysterious to fit our formulas for better living. It means that God is not our best friend, our secret lover, or our good luck charm. He is God.* [27]

THREE

Which Brings You Straightaway to SIN

Yeah, right! God is wonderful, good, all that. So, if God is so great, what went wrong? How come it's all so screwed up? How come I'm so screwed up? You've lost me here. What have I missed? Something doesn't fit. Help me!

—Chip

Chip is not alone in his cynical bluntness, perhaps just more direct. But the questions have ramifications which may well take us in far more directions than we would initially anticipate. In a sense, these questions, and our attempts to answer out of our Christian frame of reference, are perhaps the more ironic in a postmodern culture that believes that there are no absolutes and no boundaries, and where sin is only another quaint non-concept. Yet it is the very sense of lostness and isolation within the postmodern culture (Generation X and Generation Y) that makes this an urgent issue for us.

If we don't understand sin, and if we don't understand how badly the "screwup" affects all of creation, then we cannot begin to comprehend the dimensions of God's awesome *salvation*. Let's say that another way: If we don't comprehend how all-pervasive and radical *sin* is, then we will never begin to comprehend how all-encompassing and radical God's *salvation* is, in and through Jesus Christ. If, as we Christians continually proclaim, Jesus saves us from *sin,* then it is imperative from the very outset that we have a good grip on how utterly tragic that condition is. It also introduces a theme we shall pursue later: responding to Jesus (note it carefully) involves unbelievably profound changes in the way we live and think!

So I want to propose that the *knowledge of sin* is good news! The *knowledge of sin* is part of our *gospel.* It is not *sin* that is good news, mind you, but the *knowledge of sin.*

The Subversion of Shalom

Dirty word, *sin* is. It catches a lot of grief. But it is most useful in signifying that which misses the point of it all. It misses the point of God, his glory, and all that it embraces. It misses the point of God's person, God's nature, and God's sovereign good purpose. Sin, furthermore, misses the point of God's creatures: namely *us!* Sin leaves in its wake unimaginable tragedy. The *knowledge of sin* explains the confusion and discouraging brokenness of human society, human history, and our lives.

It is the awareness of this reality that also helps us come to grips with the antipathy (or embarrassment) toward God and toward the whole Christian understanding of the world and of life which meets us everyday in the American culture. That antipathy comes across in such subtle or not-so-subtle suggestions such as:

- ‣ Who needs God? I've got enough troubles on my own!
- ‣ God is not real or good. He's an embarrassing concept that we don't discuss or mention in polite society.
- ‣ Sin is a God-word that religious zealots use to try to impose their rules on others. Bad stuff happens? Sure. But trying to make everybody feel guilty with talk of sin? No, it's not sin; it's just the way things are. Nobody's perfect, for crying out loud!
- ‣ Salvation is self-fulfillment (if not self-worship). What we're

Subversive Jesus, Radical Grace

looking for is self-actualization, or even some kind of a social potential movement so that life is more harmonious for us. We're not looking for some downer like sin, or some escape like God.

▸ Our only solutions are really going to have to be accomplished by human thinking and human pursuits. We think and act to make the best out of a bad situation. We do the best we can with what we've got. We begin with a neutral mind and our own efforts, and go from there. And in our postmodern culture, if I can't cope with one unified self, then I will construct multiple selves in order to cope. Why not? So don't try to confuse the issue by introducing the idea that something is basically and cosmically awry. Such talk only confuses me.

Now then, it might not be stated quite so baldly and brashly by our acquaintances. And all of those objections may not be articulated in such neat and graphic language. At the same time, we need to remember that our culture is not congenial to the Christian way of understanding, thinking, and living in this real world. The culture is alien to God, and will continually challenge anything that questions human autonomy, even if that autonomy has brought it to the point of near total ruin. When the biblical document speaks of the "age of this cosmos,"[1] it speaks of a holistic, systemic, cosmic, and personal attempt to live and explain it all apart from any serious dealing with the God-who-is-God. It is, then, part of our task as agents of God's good news to point this out, with the intent of offering God's saving alternative to such a failed and failing understanding of it all.

Reducing God to Our Size

Do you remember in the last chapter when we spoke of creation, of Adam and Eve and the *virus* in the system (Genesis 3)? There are, in that Edenic paradise, several personalities: God the Creator, a woman and a man created in God's image (Eve and Adam), and a mysterious adversarial figure called "the serpent" (who only in later documents is identified as "that old serpent the Devil"). It is all so subtle and sophisticated. The scene was one of a perfect and complete *Shalom*. A serpent (where did he come from?)[2] becomes the slandering voice who challenges God's being and nature, as well as God's definition of the true state of things.

In this garden paradise was a symbolic planting called the "tree of good and evil." God had communicated to the man and woman that the whole garden was theirs to enjoy, was his gift to them; only the fruit of this tree was off-limits. To eat it was to introduce an alien factor into their lives which would bring about *death*. So, enter the serpent. In so many words the serpent cynically suggests: "What God says is not necessarily true! It may be good here in the garden, but it could be even better. God is not necessary to this equation! Who says that God is the one to define what is *good?* I want to redefine 'good' for you. God is keeping something from you. God is violating your rights. God is telling you to deny your valid self-expression. God is presuming to be superior to you. Don't let him get away with that. You have as much right to eat the fruit as God does to tell you not to. Eat it and you'll show God that you're his equal—you will be gods too! That is what is really 'good.'"

Oops! Loss of innocence. Virus enters the system. The cosmic screwup begins: "The whole creation groans."[3] *Evil* becomes a reality. Evil is that which is the distortion of *good,* causing creation to be experienced, and life to be pursued, without the primary relationship to the personal God. We're talking now about *sin.* The only true harmony, the only true *Shalom,* is when God is God, and when God is embraced and worshiped as such: "In thy presence [*only*] is fullness of joy, and at thy right hand [*only*] are pleasures forevermore."[4]

Chip's questions and complaints are ones with which we must come to grips. The reality of the blight demands some explanation. The Genesis account is certainly not a philosophical treatise on *theodicy,* or any theological attempt to somehow reconcile the nature of God with the presence of moral evil. Not at all. It leaves a multitude of our curious inquiries unanswered. But it *does* give us the simple and necessary clue which we need. The clue lies somewhere in the creature (creation) missing the point of God and his sovereign good purpose for creation, and a resentment by the creature of creaturely status under God, which in turn means the denial of true worship of God as being our highest *good.* A pervasive suspicion intrudes into the *Shalom.* It also begins to answer another nagging question: "If God is so good, how come he gets such a bad rap so much of the time? If God is so wonderful how come he is always becoming the fall guy for everything that goes wrong?"

Such questions are inescapable to any thoughtful person, and to the effective agents of God's good news. It is for this reason that I stated earlier that the *knowledge of sin* is good news. However, once we open that door and look in, we also have to face the reality that *sin* is far more inclusive and pervasive than just some personal "missing the point." It is that, to be sure. But the effects of sin are cosmic. Those effects saturate the daily experience of our imaginary friend Chip, his friends and ours, and all of humankind!

Still, such attempts to somehow bring God into manageable proportions are an ever-present reality in the human scene. When Eve and Adam, the crown and caretakers of God's creation, sought equality with God in the garden, things began to unravel. The challenge of the serpent was to leave God out of the equation and to substitute a new and *nontheistic* view of reality, knowledge, and behavior. It was a tragic rebellion of the creature against the Creator. God's blessings, which were the normal state of things (*Shalom*) before this point, could no longer be presumed or taken for granted. The relationship between Eve and Adam, previously perfectly beautiful, harmonious, and intimate, became strained. They accused each other and God for what had taken place, then blamed the serpent. Neither could admit that what they had done was an attempt to be set free from their creaturely role as the glory of God, nor at that point had they had any idea of the consequences of their actions.

It's no good for us to pass the buck to these primordial parents. We see the same stuff in ourselves. History from that point repeatedly demonstrates how that subversion (rebellion) left creation polluted and humankind adrift. The heirs of Adam and Eve have always tried to explain life without God. They have tried to fashion a god who could be manipulated, or was more congenial to their lifestyle, or even to explain God away as nothing more than the fabrication of the human mind to meet some inner need. When the true God is displaced, then humankind wants a god who is predictable, rational, more cozy and controllable. We sinful beings want a god who exists to meet *our* needs and bless *our* whims.

A poet put it this way: "It has been lonely in the world since God died."[5] So true! The heart of God's creatures somehow longs for its true home with God, but it is estranged. The world's religions are nothing more than an expression of our illusive need for transcendence, for deity, which gnaws on the fringes of our consciousness. The followers of Jesus must see this longing, this need, behind every expression of religion, superstition, and the occult. Even those who stridently deny God have moments when they suspect that they are far from the truth.

We see and hear the tragic emptiness in so much of any culture's music, in the quest for meaning and true love, in laments over brokenness and betrayal. The confessions of self-deception are as apparent in literature as in liturgical prayers. For example, the novels of Walker Percy probe the psychological emptiness of so many otherwise successful and familiar personalities and suggest that the real solution may be found in God. The follower of Jesus who is serious in being an agent of God's good news needs to listen and respond to these expressions.

THE DIMENSIONS OF SIN

Lest we dwell only on the individual and personal dimensions of sin, we need to be reminded that to do so reflects one of the common reductions of the gospel in the North American Christian community. When we embrace a truncated view of sin, what follows is a truncated view of the gospel! In defining sin for ourselves we face several problems:

1. An *individualistic view of sin and evil* ignores sin's systemic dimensions, not to mention the hapless victims of such systemic sin. For instance, a person can be ever so

scrupulous about his or her personal life and behavior, yet be entirely complicit in unjust and destructive systems and structures, which involve the welfare of persons who are out of sight.

2. The *enslaving, blinding, and subtly seductive power of sin,* both personally and corporately, is downplayed. We stubbornly resist acknowledging that we are hopelessly captive, slaves to sin. Like the religious leaders of Jesus' day, we may subconsciously think, "We are the descendants of Abraham, we were never in captivity to any man."[6] Even Christians resist the radical changes that New Creation calls for!

3. The tragic and disruptive reality of sin gets muted. Beyond the tragedy of personal sin is economic sin, political sin, corporate sin, contextual sin, environmental sin, intellectual sin, metaphysical sin, ethical sin, epistemological sin, national sin, ecclesiastical sin, and even theological sin—whatever misses the point of God's nature and good purpose. We'll come back to some of these later.

4. Perhaps we also need to include here some of the more immediate and tragic results of the cosmic falleness in which we share. These are obvious in the common human experience of sickness, *infirmities, and human disasters.* We ask the unanswerable questions of God's presence and power when we are experiencing these traumas more often than when we are cruising along in safety and health. These ravaging and often inexplicable times are also a part of the tragedy that sin has brought onto the human scene, and they need to be recognized as such.

To probe the full ramifications of the tragedy of sin is far beyond the scope of this book. But when we invite men and women to "follow Jesus Christ" and to receive the salvation which he offers us in the gospel, we need to know something of what that entails.

Somehow we are offering them God's deliverance, God's rescue from sin through Jesus Christ, and we dare not be superficial in understanding what that is all about. Let's review briefly a few specific examples.

PERSONAL SIN is whatever defiles or distorts the image of God's image and purpose in humankind, anything that destroys and dehumanizes one's personal life. We usually focus our attention here because it is the most immediate and obvious. Whereas God created persons to have a wholesome sense of themselves in his image, and to walk in joyous and fulfilling relationship with himself and each other, we see daily evidence that this is not true. The Bible describes such persons as being "without hope and without God in the world."[7] There is something missing at the core of these human lives. They are blind to God's purposes and captive to all kinds of distorted human desires and destructive urges.

Hopelessness is one of the most obvious present evidences of sin—life cut off from any sense of meaning. These hopeless and meaningless lives breed much of the violence and substance abuse so prevalent among us.

Meaningless existence frequently lashes out in cynicism, in criticism of anything and everything that brings discomfort into our lives. It expresses itself in driving ambition that runs over any and every obstacle, even any sense of decency. It manifests itself in personal peccadilloes as well as criminal activity. Anger, greed, dissatisfaction, lust, self-absorption, and often suicide are all evidences of something tragically wrong. We long for self-improvement but don't know where or how to look for it. It is in this personal sin and lostness that we live with our vain quests for the pursuit of happiness, our equally vain attempts at self-actualization, and the protectiveness of our "rights." We are torn between our befuddling desires for both aloneness and for community. When we are by ourselves we ponder our experience of being "lost in the cosmos."[8] This personal sense of disconnectedness from anything larger than ourselves, and the failure to find the heart's true home, are where we all begin to understand the scope of sin.

Subversive Jesus, Radical Grace

INTERPERSONAL SIN is whatever erodes God's true purpose in human community; in other words, true intimacy, true caring, true dignity. Look around. Our autonomous natures, while longing for intimacy and wholesome relationships, are unable to achieve them. The evidence of interpersonal sin shows up in the erosion of both the nuclear family as well as the neighborhood community. Divorce, child abuse, spousal abuse, family violence, dysfunctionality in relationships, and autonomous individuals dwelling under one roof are more and more the norm. This results in all kinds of pathologies within the larger community. When our own sense of self cannot relate to other selves purposefully and positively, then true community tends to dissolve.

C. S. Lewis uses his fecund imagination to describe hell as a "gray city" in which people live in mutual isolation from each other, in proximity but distanced from any real relationships.[9] This is what has too often come to pass in the demise of wholesome neighborhoods in American culture. Individuals respond to the allure of something called "suburbs" where they have little occasion for relating to others. To be sure, there may be contrived sociability, or "cocktail hour superficiality," but such are not true community. Privatism prevails. Anger erupts when anything intrudes to disturb our protected space.

We hope to satisfy our longings through multiple marriages, recreational and casual sexual liaisons, superficial associations such as chat rooms, virtual sex, health clubs, or sports bars. In such settings we can hide behind our carefully poised personas, moats constructed around our citadels of inner emptiness and lack of identity. Even Christian churches can be a demonstration of such gatherings of nameless bodies who have no sense of group identity or of responsibility or accountability to anyone else.

On the world scene we have seen those who profess to be Protestant Christians killing those who profess to be Catholic Christians (Ireland). Or Christians killing Christians (Rwanda). Elsewhere, we have seen those who profess to be Christians engaged in the "ethnic cleansing" of those who should be the objects of Christ's redemptive mission, namely their Islamic neighbors (Bosnia).

In the last chapter we reviewed the Ten Commandments as an expression of God's good concern for humankind. When we fail to love God's creation—whether in our own families or the families around us—we commit sin. To view others as annoyances, inconveniences, threats, even as enemies because of their ethnic identity, strange tongues, or economic and social differences shows how far we have fallen from God's true *Shalom*.

SYSTEMIC SIN is that which we hardly notice because we are formed by it and accept it as normal. Yet it is a very real evil that can intimidate us to the point of despair. Systemic sin has to do with all of those power structures, those forces "out there" that determine our lives whether we like it or not, or whether we are even conscious of them. Systemic sin emerges frequently in the Bible under the rubric of principalities and powers. One writer described the principalities and powers as being any institution of humankind (however well-intended) which demands for itself a devotion which belongs only to God.[10] What we're talking about here is a subtle loyalty which influences to its advantage all other loyalties.

This is nowhere more apparent than in development of American cities, which have developed into unbelievably impersonal environments.[11] In the quest for progress, we have created cities without community, communities without neighborhoods, neighborhoods without neighbors. We have communities without sidewalks, where one is totally captive without an automobile. Automobiles have become our private means of zooming from one location to another without any significant interpersonal contact (other than an occasional wave or obscene digital signal).

We have created what one sociologist described as the "sterile, impersonal everywhereness of shopping malls," where strangers walk and mingle amid stores owned by corporations whose owners are headquartered half a continent away, and care only for the bottom line. That I am a customer with a name is of little significance. A person can be desperately lonely in the midst of five million people!

Perhaps I am being a bit harsh, but the disastrous condition of much of urban America is a terrible indictment on the Christian

Subversive Jesus, Radical Grace

church's too-often abrogation of any responsibility to be the community of God's New Creation in Jesus Christ. We accept the *system* without discernment. We become part of the systemic sin rather than being the people of the New Creation who are a redemptive force seeking the welfare "of the city in where I have sent you."[12]

Another not-so-subtle evidence of systemic sin is the whole economic structure in which we live. Impersonal corporations appear to be ruled by a sophisticated greed, which has little sense of responsibility to individuals other than stockholders. Company policy becomes absolute. It can create wealthy executives with huge stock options, exploit workers, downsize and disrupt families, devastate the environment, and destabilize smaller countries and economies, all in the name of "economic health." Some corporations can ignore any sense of responsibility for the larger community except that which enhances their own corporate image. Those who are economically powerless hardly register in the corporate planning and sense of responsibility of these entities.

It is quite easy for us to be blind to this, accept it, even justify it as *practical reality!* But more than most of us realize, we are too much formed by it. The huge advertising industry is part and parcel of this phenomenon. This industry exacerbates our greed and creates the very real religion of *consumerism.* Even churches can fall into the trap, becoming economic enterprises modeling their success after the corporate image. They can advertise their "success" at the expense of faithfulness, or any relation to the mission of God. Churches can become part of the *system!*

Somewhere in this systemic consideration lie the corporate idolatries which form our lives and that dare us to challenge them. Among such idolatries are national*ism,* American*ism,* militar*ism,* and capital*ism.* Each one can be purposeful in God's *Shalom,* but each can all too easily take on a life of its own and become detrimental to the same. At this writing we are engaged in many policies that destroy lives around the world under the rationale of "American interests abroad." When we refuse to adopt a ban on land mines, or we economically boycott nations in order to punish their leaders, we cause innocent and helpless people to suffer. We also have convenient and selective memories about our complicity in episodes of genocide in our own national history.

Our systems can create homelessness. Our medical technology can make it quite simple to perform abortions and other ethically questionable procedures. Technology itself is an idol of frightening proportions. This is not to mention all of the other idolatries that become *isms,* such as sex*ism,* rac*ism,* and class*ism.*

Environmental violation likewise deserves attention. For some of our postmodern friends who don't recognize sin anywhere else, they do here! One of the alarming results of systemic sin and technological sin is the callousness with which God's creation is being destroyed by toxic wastes, exploitation of the natural environment, fouling of water sources, and depletion of the ozone layer, to name a few. Often these actions are justified in the name of progress, or technological advances! We are all influenced.

Systemic sin is a Pandora's box of dehumanizing and destructive patterns with which we have become so comfortable and captive that we hardly notice. This is the *world* from which we are called, and to which we are sent back, but also warned not to be conformed to. To come to Jesus is to be challenged, to be changed into a New Creation, and to be made into a redemptive subversive in alien systems![13]

THE DEMONIC FACTOR. We must acknowledge the mystery of Satan, but this malignant personality is right there energizing the darkness. The prayer of Jesus petitions: "Deliver us from the evil one." The apostle John declares that "the whole world lies in the evil one."[14] What's going on here? The modern era essentially discounted any idea of Satan, or of the supernatural forces of evil and darkness. The idea of any demonic activity in this "rational world" was looked down upon as quaint and certainly not worthy of being taken seriously. It still is a perilous subject to be raised in much of the theological academy! But there is a reality here that will not go away.

Ironically, in this postmodern culture the bookstores are full of books on witchcraft, spirit worship, and such evidences of the occult. While some may deride the idea, the culture knows something that scholars may have missed. Jesus and the apostles spoke candidly about the prince of this world, the devil, the evil one, the liar and the murderer, the accuser of our sisters and brothers in Christ.[15]

Satan (or whatever name he takes) is not at all sovereign, but he is supernatural, and he is real. There are many destructive things in our lives and society that defy rational explanation. They resist the best of our human solutions. This Adversary is not some ridiculous figure in red tights. Quite the opposite. Satan is sophisticated and clever and shrewd and a master of disguise, coming as an "angel of light." Nothing makes this more apparent to us at this point in history than the fact that Europe and North America, which have had more exposure to the gospel than any other parts of the world, are now the two most resistant cultures to the gospel. How a culture could build up "antibodies" to the love and grace of God with such skill is mind-boggling. It is demonic!

The modern era effectively discounted this reality, with its optimistic assessment of human potential and the inevitability of progress. And the church bought into this optimism, so much so that even evangelism becomes nothing more than a marketing technique or a human scheme to "build the kingdom," which totally discounts the mandate given to the apostle:

> *I send you to open their eyes, that they may turn from darkness to light and from the power of Satan to God, that they may receive forgiveness of sins and a place among those who are sanctified by faith in me.*[16]

AND ALL THE OTHER EXPRESSIONS OF SIN. In missing the point of God and his glory, in leaving God out of the equation, the creation is subject to bondage and is blighted by the pathological presence of so many diverse expressions of this tragedy. We continually are subject to the riptides of secular gospels, and the *zeitgeists* of popular trends and fads which seduce us away from the point of it all. These are like the treacherous Molokai Channel between the Hawaiian Islands—you may know that you shouldn't have gotten into it in the first place, and you may wish you could go back, but there's no hope. So it is with the expressions of sin. But, having made the point of how tragic and radical is the reality of sin, we need to always remember that none of it is beyond remedy.

The Hapless and Helpless Victims of Sin

All that we have been describing thus far also has its victims, those who not by their own choice, but by their helplessness of time and place and circumstance, have been scarred by the *virus*. These people have not chosen where they were born, or the context of their lives. These are the trapped, the crushed, the dehumanized, the despairing, the ignored, the trivialized, the violated . . . those for whom the Spirit anointed Jesus, and anoints us, to bring good news. The church tends to focus on our individual sin, or evil. We also do a reasonable job of seeing the evidence of interpersonal evil. Occasionally we get prophetic and raise our voices against systemic sin and evil. But if we are to be faithful evangelists, we must look carefully at how much of the biblical material, and the life and teachings of Jesus, speak to the very real and tragic reality of those who are the totally helpless victims of the *chaos*, of the systemic sin and evil of this human scene.

Does the joyous news of God's Dominion have any bearing on evil systems and their victims? Everything in the Bible cries: "Yes!" Jesus looked upon the needy multitudes and had compassion. Though the answers are difficult and costly, famine, genocide, urban poverty, AIDS, drug addiction, child and spousal abuse cannot be looked upon by God's New Creation people with indifference. To do so is perilous. One has only to look at Jesus' own teaching about his coming at the end of this age, and his separation of sheep (those who love him) from goats (those who don't).[17] The criteria? Ministry to the hungry, homeless, naked, sick, and imprisoned. Is such ministry *gospel*? Is such human helplessness part of our understanding of sin? One has to be blind and deaf to the ministry and teachings of Jesus to think otherwise!

Total Depravity and Common Grace

Which brings us to another challenge and question from the Chips of our acquaintance:

*Get real! All you're talking about is the bad stuff and the neg-
atives of this life. Sure, there's a lot that's screwed up in this
life. But then if it's so totally screwed up, how come there is so
much good in a lot of people, in relationships, and in the system? Aren't you painting a pretty bleak picture?*

In passing, this objection needs to be addressed but not dwelt
upon. Yes, everything in all creation suffers the effects of the tragedy,
the pervasive blight and visible depravity, of human rebellion against
the Creator. Again, "the whole creation groans." But it is still the
sovereign purpose of the Creator God that his glory be evidenced
in the whole of it. So we live with the twin realities that: (1) it all
falls short of God's design and glory, but (2) God is good, and in his
goodness he still preserves his creation from its self-destructive bent.
God sends the rain upon the just and the unjust. God bestows his
common grace (gifts), or *preserving grace,* upon his creation so that it
always has some hope and beauty, even in its darker expressions.

Persons who are absolutely godless can produce works of beauty
and benefit. Pagans, who flagrantly object to any mention of God,
can be the instruments of justice and peace even though they do
not know from where these urges come.[18] Relationships and systems
can be used to produce caring and provision even when God's being
is unknown or denied.

Which is to say that just because the creature has denied the
Creator, and just because the whole creation is blighted, does not
mean that God has abandoned what is his own, or is asleep at the
switch, or has thrown in the towel. Depravity is our contribution
to the scene, but *common grace* is God's good intrusion in even the
most unlikely places, and in the most unlikely persons or systems!
This raises another obvious question.

Are There Consequences?
Judgment, Hell, and All That

Chip asks, "So what if I blow off all this you've been saying? Who
cares? What difference does it make?"

Yes, there is an insistent question which forces itself on us at this juncture in our discussion. There is a difficult and delicate issue that we must raise to visibility. We should not proceed without coming to grips with the *consequences* of rejecting God, his agenda, and his free offer of grace and love in Jesus Christ! Any sensitive Christian will entertain this question with great humility, compassion, and sensitivity. The question which arises is this: What happens to those who either don't know of, or else adamantly reject God's infinite love made known in Christ? Or what happens to those nasty, destructive, arrogant folk who mess up life for so many others? Or, again, what happens to those who repeatedly hear the gospel but never seem to get the message or take it seriously, and never come to Jesus Christ for true transformation? As uncomfortable as the whole subject is, it won't go away that easily. Any grappling with the disciplines of evangelism will, sooner or later, have to include these questions.

First, let's establish a foundational New Testament principle: Jesus said, "For God sent the Son into the world, not to condemn the world, but that the world might be saved through him."[19] This is promising. It lets us know, first of all, that God's primary agenda is not to *zap* every person who is wicked. Rather, God's primary agenda, out of his infinite love and good purpose for his whole creation, is that it all be reconciled, that the whole creation be brought again into the relationship with himself that is true *Shalom,* and so become a reflection of the Creator, God's *glory.* God's agenda, as given to Abraham, is that in his seed "all the nations of the earth shall be blessed."[20]

The problem is this: the *world* and its inhabitants are already part of the judgment! The same passage from the Gospel of John goes on: "He who believes in him is not condemned; he who does not believe is [part of the condemnation] already, because he has not believed in the name of the only Son of God."[21] The *world* (κοσμος) is one biblical name for the whole created scene in its *missing-the-point* condition, as it rejects the Author of true life and reality. To live apart from the Creator (and especially the Anointed Son and Rescuer, Jesus) is to inhabit the *Death,* in other words, to be "condemned already."

Subversive Jesus, Radical Grace

According to this passage, *light* has come into the world, but men and women don't want the *light* because it exposes what they don't want to have known. Hiding from God has been going on since the episode in the Garden of Eden when God asked Adam and Eve that first evangelistic question, "Where are you?" The *condemnation* is that we, as humankind, reject God and so reject the Author of life, the Giver of life's true being. This also means that we do not even know who we are. We are dishonest with ourselves. Then, we are suspicious of others lest they make demands upon our autonomy. We hide from each other and do things that we don't want to be brought to the *light*. We think thoughts, and engage in practices, and approve principles that violate what God intends for his creation. In short, we are already part of the darkness, the lostness, the condemnation—a life without God.

God takes very seriously all that is not in sync with who he is and what he created it for. If sin is not tragic, or if God is not angry with the violation of his creation and the wickedness of humankind, then somehow the Cross of Jesus seems a bit overdone, even a tragicomedy. If it took his one and only Son to bear all of the consequences of the human and cosmic rebellion, it certainly proves that God does not trivialize our screwups, our sinfulness.

As if that weren't enough, then we have to face up to the biblical teaching that Jesus, who came once as God's word of love and grace in flesh and blood, has promised to come a second time in power and great glory to judge, and to establish righteousness. Part of our message is that "we shall all [Christians as well as nonChristians] stand before the judgment throne of Christ to give answer for the deeds done in the body."[22] Everything will be brought into the light, all will be naked and exposed before the Son of God.

The book of Revelation, at one point, portrays Jesus Christ with "eyes like flames of fire."[23] The very prospect of our being totally revealed, dragged out of all of our hiding places, into stark public nakedness before infinite holiness is not a comfortable thought—apart from the grace and love of Jesus Christ to the repentant and believing. In the presence of Christ the Judge we are going to have all that is unholy and unbelieving purged out of us by the refining fire of God's holiness.[24] However all of this comes about, ultimately nothing will remain that is not in complete oneness and harmony with the holiness and majesty and love of God: "All flesh shall see his glory."

At this point what we are likely to hear is a cynical protest:

So maybe that's my choice. Maybe I'll take my chances. So I screw it up, and I die. What then? I'm dead. I've blown it. But at least the pain and uncertainties of this life are done and behind me. What else is there?

Such a response is sheer nihilism. It assumes that all of life amounts to nothing. "Eat, drink, and indulge yourself, for tomorrow you die!" Such a completely self-indulgent and nihilistic view of life, please note, is also a very real *faith position!* It stands in a stark, collision-course difference with our Christian faith, which says that we can't escape God that easily.

The question remains: What happens to those who don't buy in to God's unbelievable good news? To be honest, the Bible *appears* to provide two different sets of answers that don't always seem to fit. One set of answers says that there really is an everlasting punishment for the unbelievers, the wicked, the immoral, the practitioners of injustice, the worshipers of idols, and all of those things that violate and offend God and God's good purpose for his creation. But then there is another set of answers, for example in 2 Peter 3:9, that speaks of God as "not willing that any should perish, but that all should come to God." There are biblical texts which speak of every knee bowing and every tongue confessing that Jesus Christ is Lord. Such would indicate that nobody who doesn't ultimately share in this worship is permanently left in some lake of fire!

The church has always struggled with this mystery, and so do we.[25] The Bible speaks out of many different historical settings, in many literary forms, in narrative and metaphor. Yet all are pieces of the picture which form our understanding. They are also part of the mystery.

THE UNCOMFORTABLE NEWS. We need to acknowledge these seemingly contradictory portrayals in the Bible. But the incontrovertible message in biblical documents is that God is a righteous judge who expresses wrath at the violations of his design; that somehow and ultimately wicked men and women will vanish from the scene.[26] There is a context of fiery destruction called hell. To spend one's life in the service of that which is alien to God's design pays frightening wages. Many Scriptures speak of such, enough to get our full and sober attention, in spades![27] But the Scriptures also speak of other realities, and with a different tone that must also be taken into consideration and held firmly.

THE TRUE COMFORT OF OUR GOSPEL. The Scriptures reveal that God is a God who pardons sin and forgives iniquity and who will not stay angry forever, but delights to show mercy; that Jesus Christ is ultimately the one who reconciles the whole world; that in Jesus Christ, God reconciles the world to himself; that Jesus Christ is the propitiation for our sins (the recipient of God's holy wrath against sin on our behalf), and not for ours only but also for the sins of the whole world; that ultimately God is going to make *all things* new, and will wipe away all tears, and death shall be no more; and that (and this is the enigmatic word) ultimately death and Hades will be thrown into the destroying fire![28, 29]

"WELL?" Many of us have been provoked into another dimension of consideration by the British World War I chaplain-poet G. A. Studdert-Kennedy. He has written a very poignant poem entitled "Well?" in which a British soldier, replete with his limey accent, is musing over his chaplain's sermons about Judgment Day, the great white throne: *"And 'ow each chap would 'ave to stand, and answer on 'is own."* He rummages through his careless life and all of the lousy things he had gotten into, and the hurtful things he had done. Then he dreams he is dead and standing before Jesus, the judge of all. He sees the infinite love and grace of Jesus for just such messed-up, ordinary folk as himself and is reduced to infinite grief. He concludes in some agony:

There ain't no throne, and there ain't no books,
    It's 'Im, just 'Im you've got to see,
It's 'Im, just 'Im, that is the Judge
    Of blokes like you and me.
And boys, I'd sooner frizzle up,
    I' the flames of a burnin' 'Ell,
Than stand and look into 'Is face,
    And 'ear 'Is voice say — "Well?" [30]

Let's face it: We do not know how God's purpose to bring everything in all of creation to his glory, to bring the ultimate *Shalom*, will unfold. At the same time there are some things that we know right well. We know that *everything* is created by and for Jesus Christ. We know that by him all things are made and by him they are held together.[31] Somehow to reject Jesus is to ultimately reject any possibility of *being*. We know that life without God is futile, hopeless, and even meaningless in and of itself.

We also know that on the cross, Jesus suffered that ultimate abandonment, being forsaken by God. And existence without God is true hell. Jesus experienced separation from God to its infinite depths. He "drank the cup" of the wrath of God. We know that he did this so that we could be restored into the unbelievably intimate, infinitely beautiful, and completely perfect relationship with God the Father which has no barriers and no misgivings. We know that he did this "for the joy set before him."[32] We know that what he did for us makes us true sons and daughters of God. But we also know that, like Studdert-Kennedy's soldier mused, we are all going to have to look into Jesus' eyes.

We also know that *hell* is not some impersonal reality of pain and suffering apart from the reality of the Person of the Holy God. Ultimately, everything exists by and for Jesus, and has no existence without his upholding hand and his life-giving breath. Ultimately, every person will certainly meet the Crucified God who is the Righteous Judge of All. It is like C. S. Lewis recalling his conversion experience: "I heard the footsteps of Him whom I so desperately did not want to meet!"[33] Or like Studdert-Kennedy's soldier, we will look

Subversive Jesus, Radical Grace

into the eyes of flaming fire in the Lamb and hear him say, "Well?"

And that's the *hell* of it! And no one escapes. But this is part of our message—and part of our uncomfortable gospel. Beyond all of the unanswered questions lingers the assurance from Holy Scriptures: "Will not the Judge of all the earth do right?"[34] Yes! And the Judge of all is Jesus the Lamb, and the Lamb is Jesus the Judge. Our task is to be those faithful ambassadors of God who invite and implore men and women to find in Jesus their heart's true home. He came to rescue us from all the consequences of subversion, of sin. And he came to inaugurate the New Creation which is *Shalom*. He will not fail nor be discouraged until he has established justice in the earth.

Lostness and Compassion: From Hell to Hope

*So here's all of this sin and hell stuff. Here is what
you call a "subversion" of what God intended. Yeah,
right! So, closer to home, we've got an existential "hell"
which leaves us without light, without hope, without
meaning, without truth, without direction; at the mercy
of powers we don't comprehend and can't control.
So we are at the mercy of our hormones, greed, ill-
founded expectations, all kinds of irrational and
destructive "zeitgeists," our addictions, the irreversibil-
ity of aging and death, not to mention the stuff in the
community and nation that is too discouraging to deal
with. We are at the mercy of all the emotions that
go along with these: our fears, our cynicism, our guilt,
and our uncertainty. So here we are stuck with **I am**,
and **we are**, and who knows why? Or even cares?
So what have you got to say to all of that?*

—Chip

Hell, for most of our friends, is a much more immediate and
closer-at-hand reality. Their daily nightmares are not about
some far-off future confrontation with the living God so much as
the inescapably hollow existence of each day.

If we are to be the agents of God's reconciling love in the here and now, we are not dealing with theoretical or hypothetical persons. Rather, we are dealing with acquaintances, with friends and neighbors who live with the confusion and frustration of lives disconnected from their Creator, and hence from their heart's true home. This produces an *existential hell* which hides behind the current fashions but is just as real and agonizing. One has only to note the escalating suicide rate among teenagers or listen to their music to be aware of this.[1]

The problems we face, then, are on one hand, how to so *evangelize* (make urgent and thrilling and compelling) the message of Jesus for those *outside;* and on the other, how to so *evangelize* those of us who are *inside,* the on-the-scene agents of that message, who get complacent and indifferent. How can we engage our ministry of God's good news so that it emerges out of some kind of joyous and passionate *gut-response* for these real people who are still outside, still *lost?* The very reality of human lostness is not some theological abstraction. Rather it is what called forth the compassion of Jesus, and so must with us.

I once taught evangelism to a seminary class and ran head-on into this dilemma. Those students who had come from *outside,* who were adult converts to Jesus Christ, had a very real and instant identification with what we were teaching. They remembered their own pilgrimage out of lostness. On the other hand, those students who had grown up *inside* the Christian community, and in Christian homes, simply could not begin to get their heads and hearts into *lostness* because they had never experienced it! They had never known real *lostness!* The subject of evangelism for them was all very theoretical. They never really connected with the course.[2] But the adult converts remembered the *hell* of being without God and without hope. Lostness is, in itself, a very real *hell.*

The fact that some Christian folk are unable to comprehend (or care) that others are really lost, and for those outside to not be persuaded that they *are* lost, puts a wide gulf between the two. Such absence of any intense compassion and love on the part of Christian folk almost eliminates any motivation to be urgent bearers of God's good news.

Subversive Jesus, Radical Grace

Consider this: We will find some persons *outside* who are open and searching and looking for God's answer to their inner emptiness. Some will try to put together a *do-it-yourself-god,* a "designer god," fabricated out of many philosophies to bring them to some kind of "self-actualization."[3] But more often we find those who not only don't have a clue about their *lostness,* but also don't really care.

LOST IN THE 'HOOD

Our friends like Chip tend to respond to the cultural neighborhood (the 'hood) in which they have grown up. Persons are blinded and captive to the fashions, expectations, prevailing thought patterns, social pressures, and mass culture around them—in other words, the "powers" of this age. They are participants in a community that leaves God out of the equation. Add to this the confession that we are all heirs of the cosmic rebellion against the Creator, and we're left with a cosmic "separation anxiety."

We have all encountered the kind of folk who live on the periphery of society, whose lives and instincts and appetites are little more than animal-like: survive, have fun, have sex, go deer hunting, get drunk, make a little money to do more of the same. God and ultimate questions are the last thing on their minds. They are so dehumanized by circumstances or choice that it is near impossible to get through to them on any significant level beyond what they are experiencing.

At the opposite end of the spectrum are "upper-class" folk who are also so lost in, and dehumanized by, their circumstances and the social ethos that have forced them into a lifestyle that has no meaning above satisfying the vanity of their existence. Many of these social elite cruise along as pawns of their pride, appetites, and fads, with the mindless assumption that this is simply the way things are. Their neighborhood of lostness is elegant but just as hellish. These people also are the objects of God's compassionate heart.

But most obvious and familiar is the middle-class, mass-market culture of North America. These folk generally dwell in a cultural neighborhood drowning in materialism and consumerism. Their emptiness is totally fashionable: Go to the same malls, covet the same things, listen to the same music, watch the same inane television shows, go to the popular movies, be addicted to the same consumer seductions, and wear the same market-driven styles. Our suburbanite acquaintances strive after similar career and financial goals, in hopes of gaining security and early retirement. They join the same clubs and engage in the same leisure as everybody else as though this is the "good life."

They have also created a huge therapy industry to try to resolve the emptiness that these things and activities don't fill. No matter the socioeconomic status, these are all real persons, the objects of God's love, created in his image. When the Bible describes persons as being "dead in their trespasses and sins," it is descriptive of the life that is so much a part of the mass culture: "In all his thoughts there is no room for God."[4]

The question comes: What are the issues, the questions that all humankind ponder in the silences of their lives? What answers would constitute the ultimate *good news* to them?

THE QUESTIONS

What answers would, indeed, constitute the ultimate good news? What are the questions that expose the dimensions of darkness and lostness? Here are a few:

- Does anything connect with *anything?*
- Is there "something" that could be defined as *reality?*
- Who am I? Is there something that I can identify as *self?*
- Does this life have any meaning?
- Is there anything ultimate out there that can be called *God?*
- If so, what kind of being is he/she/it?
- If so, how does he/she/it relate to me? Does he/she/it know I exist? Or like me? Or care?
- What if I don't measure up?
- How do I know, discern, or measure *truth?* Is there *light* in this screwed-up darkness?

- Is the grave the end? Is suicide a good option to this meaningless emptiness?
- Is there some future which I haven't computed?
- Is there any way to break out of the loneliness and isolation and find some intimacy, some community, some relationships—something other than this superficial community of strangers?
- How do we live and find our way through the hell of this life with some sense of peace and purpose?
- How would I know if I were in sync with or pleasing to *God?*
- If I saw (even in the shadows) something of a different life, a New Creation, how would I ever be empowered to live such a New Creation, given my affinity for the present, and my inability to even live up to my own ideals?

It is such *questions behind the questions* that reflect the human longing for the transcendent, and the *image of God* that still exists somewhere in the human heart of the totally despairing, even in the most callous and self-sufficient. He could be our Chip. She could be the scion of a prominent family. He could be a middle-class latchkey kid, the product of divorce or overly busy parents. She could be the product of a "Joe-six-pack" sexual liaison.

All of these questions reflect that condition which the Bible poignantly describes as being *lost.* It is this tragic distortion of God's purpose for the crown of his creation that caused Jesus to look upon the multitudes and have *compassion* on them, even weep! Compassion must be our hallmark as well.

GOD COMES TO US _____

All of the world religions reflect some legitimate quest after God, after answers, after the transcendent. But in each one it is the lost creature seeking the Creator.

The God who comes into our history in Jesus is uniquely *other!* He *comes to us.* God in Christ comes into our history and into our lives seeking us. Jesus comes into the context of our human confusion, lostness, brokenness—our existential *hells*. God joins us where we are to make himself known, to show us the way, to reveal his heart and purpose for us and all creation.

"AS THE FATHER HAS SENT ME, EVEN SO DO I SEND YOU."

Jesus told his followers that he was sending them to be about the very mission that the Father had given to him.[5] This makes it imperative that we keep a very clear focus on God's passionate and redemptive love for this world and its inhabitants. God's sons and daughters are to have their Father's rescuing passion for humankind, for those who are separated from him, from his infinite goodness and love, from their heart's true home. It is the Father-God's compassion for a world which has sought to exclude him from its equation (except in emergencies!) that sends his Son, Jesus, to find these lost children and bring them back to the waiting Father. This work is the Father's joy, it is the Son's joy, and it is to be our joy!

What does it mean, then, when we who call ourselves by the name of Jesus express a tacit indifference to those who are still outside of the Father's family, still lost? Somehow, it indicates *our incomplete conversion* to Jesus. Because if Christ is in us by his Spirit, then we know that he is never indifferent. We need, then, to reexamine the completeness of our own relationship to Jesus because he came to seek and to save just such men and women.

I am willing to belabor this point because it is so basic in our pursuit of evangelistic faithfulness. It is the very joy of accomplishing such a salvation that motivated Jesus to undergo the agonizing price he paid. Consider that the rejection and hostility he endured, the misunderstanding, the noncomprehension even of his closest friends, were all overshadowed by his *compassion* for these people whom he came to seek and to save. The agony of his execution was overshadowed by the great joy that it would be to see the Father glorified in this New Creation, to see the Father's heart made glad in the return of his prodigal sons and daughters.

Subversive Jesus, Radical Grace

It is with these very screwed-up, broken, misdirected, arrogant, guilty, destructive—you name it—people with whom we rub elbows every day that we must get real! It is these persons that Jesus came to call back to their heart's true home, and to the waiting Father: "I came not to call the righteous, but sinners"; "The Son of Man . . . is a friend of [the most despised and despicable] tax collectors and sinners"; "The Son of Man came to seek and save the lost."[6] These *lost* folk are not some impersonal statistics of our church growth strategy.

One of the tragedies of the Christian enterprise in North America is that we have lost the mission-driven compassion that is at the very heart of God. We can become so focused on our own congregational life and institutional success that we can view the masses of human beings with an indifference to their heart-rending *lostness.* A first step for us in remedying this is to have our eyes and hearts open to really care, to always be on the alert for, sensitive to, identifying with, finding places of friendship with those *outside,* those who are seeking, those who are, yes, *lost!*

It is the anticipation of the pleasure and joy of the Father-God that is also part of our visceral response to seeking those who are lost. God is pleased and rejoiced, and even sings, over those who are returned to his Fatherly embrace. It was because of this identification with the Father that Jesus was a friend of sinners and scandalized the "religious" by socializing with such folk.

The apostle Paul speaks of compassion for the lost in a different vein. In talking about our ministry of reconciliation, of being God's ambassadors here in the midst of the human scene, he points out the motivation behind it all. He explains that the *love of Christ* is so overwhelming and all-consuming that we have no choice but to make it known. He then goes on to explain that because this is so, we no longer evaluate anyone by merely human standards, or worldly wisdom. Rather we see right through all of the facades, the hiding places, the reputations . . . to the lost creation of God. Then we implore them, for Christ's sake, to be reconciled to the waiting Father-God.

But what if that lost person is a real pain? Persons living in darkness can be so very difficult or distasteful in appearance and behavior that our first response is: "Forget it!" They may treat us with disdain, with prideful autonomy, with suspicion, with total ignorance and indifference, with arrogant self-sufficiency, with condescending intellectualism, with ribald guffaws or crude threats and signs, or with hostility. Some will counter that all religions are the way to God, or that all religion is a scam. Perhaps they have been burned by religion once and don't even want to get close to anything that resembles it again. Most are just so preoccupied with other "urgent" things that any consideration of God's love is number eleven on their list of "one to ten."

No! Our obedience as God's compassionate ambassadors does not depend on a warm and ready response. Not everyone will be as open as Chip to discuss spiritual issues. We may meet with enough boredom or anger or noncomprehension to pour cold water all over our zeal. It is only as our compassion sees behind the facade, behind the obtuse or defiant or sophisticated cover, that we discern that God rejoices to bring light where the darkness is the greatest. C. S. Lewis puts it thus:

> *There are no ordinary people. You have never talked to a mere mortal. . . . But it is immortals whom we joke with, work with, marry, snub, and exploit — immortal horrors or everlasting splendors. . . . Next to the Blessed Sacrament itself, your neighbor is the holiest object presented to your senses.*[7]

The love of Christ leaves us no choice!

LOSTNESS COMES UNDER MANY GUISES

If *sin* is missing the point of it all, missing the point of the Creator and of true *Shalom*, then *lostness* is experiencing life that has missed the point and so has no ultimate center. Lostness is being totally "at sea" and seeking to cope with it all using only our own human resources (which prove ultimately inadequate). Depending on who we are and in what context our lives develop, this lostness becomes obvious in many different sizes and shapes, and we will now consider a few.

Religious Lostness

We sometimes have to remind ourselves that religious lostness just may be the most prevalent expression of lostness, though not the only expression. In North American polls, most people believe in "god" by some definition. Most believe in some form of life after death, which they resist thinking about. New cults and quasi-Christian groups are continually appearing (and disappearing) and attracting to themselves folk looking for something. Other world religions are now no longer halfway around the world, but have temples right in town. Go to the religion section of any bookstore and you will find myriad expressions of the religious quest, from the bizarre and occult to the sophisticated and philosophical. Persons who have missed the point have a way of looking for whatever "the point" is!

We need to remember that it was the religious folk of Israel who did not comprehend Jesus' ministry and so were complicit in his execution. It was the religions in Ephesus and in the Grecian cities that harassed Paul's apostolic ministry. The darkness that causes folk to be lost is very often quite religious, but hostile to the true Light.

One can even be a tenured church member, theologically trained, and still lost! Abraham Kuyper, a brilliant theologian who ultimately became prime minister of the Netherlands, was a young clergyman when challenged in his lostness and unbelief by a simple peasant woman in his first parish. Folk in churches can become comfortable in the familiar church ethos, enjoy the music, like the people, feel secure in the traditions and the gospel words . . . and altogether miss the point of Jesus Christ, never knowing new life in him. Religious lostness does not yet know that, in Jesus, God is manifest in the flesh, and that in him grace and truth are made known.

Metaphysical Lostness

We spoke earlier of metaphysical sin. Now we need to see it in its human expression. Generations X and Y are generational cultures to whom ethical absolutes are pretty shadowy. For them something larger than "right and wrong" obsesses their lives. These men and women want to know: What is the big picture? They have this haunting question about whether or not there is *any meaning at all,* or *anything ultimate* out there which somehow will give purpose to their lives adrift. One of the most heartbreaking descriptions of lostness in the New Testament is: "without hope and without God in the world."[8] I can think of no more poignant expression of metaphysical lostness.

Metaphysical lostness does not yet know that everything was created by and for Jesus Christ and that he alone is the Alpha and Omega of all creation, that in him all things have meaning and take on focus.

Epistemological Lostness

Integrally related to the metaphysical expression of lostness is that lostness which has no criteria for what is true and what is not. Endless philosophical constructs chase this subject all over the landscape: "Truth is relative." "Truth is a human construct of convenience." "There is no truth." "Truth is whatever works." Postmodern philosophers are even more cynical about the possibility of truth. But this philosophical darkness filters down into the pop culture and becomes the lurking uncertainty which intensifies the darkness. When one is being assaulted by endless claims of fulfillment or meaning, and when nonstop advertisements guarantee some kind of utopian existence, then folk have every right to dismiss all claims with understandable cynicism because there is no standard of ultimate truth in their darkness.

When God is left out of the equation, one is consigned to the boundless sea of chance. This lostness does not yet know that the God of Truth has spoken. Much less does it acknowledge that in Jesus the Truth has been made flesh and blood, and that his words are Spirit and Truth.

Ethical Lostness

It is very possible that at the dawn of a new century, we confront the darkness most visibly in ethical lostness. When society jettisons any common understanding of transcendence, especially of the God of Abraham, Isaac, and Jacob, the God and Father of our Lord Jesus Christ, then the residual cultural influence of that faith may endure for a time, but ultimately truth and error, right and wrong, become purely relative, subjective, fluid, interchangeable! For Generation X, there are, tragically, no absolutes and no basis for establishing right and wrong except that which is currently fashionable. Rights replace absolutes. Self-actualization displaces ethics. Fornication (for example) becomes a right, even an acceptable bit of recreation, but environmental pollution to this generation is a no-no! To any insistence on behavioral standards comes the response: "Who says?" Without some ultimate God-created *Shalom,* we are left on our own to determine how to live and find fulfillment. The biblical teaching of sin and righteousness become indecipherable. This *lostness* meets us at every turn.

Spiritual Lostness

Related to all the others is the vague but insistent sense that something is incomplete. As Pascal stated, there is a God-shaped vacuum in every person. This haunting sense of incompleteness may express itself in depressing guilt or compulsive behavior, even hopelessness. But it is real. Its reality operates symbiotically with every other expression of lostness, as well as intellectual blindness, moral bondage, not to mention such things as substance abuse, juvenile violence, or other destructive patterns of behavior. Lost is *lost.* We are created by and for God, and when that reality is forfeited, life just doesn't work!

FIVE

Jesus: The Return of Shalom

What does Jesus have to do with anything?
—Chip

Shalom is the "heart's true home." It is that profound and ecstatic and harmonious intimacy with God himself, for which he made us, and flowing from which is a harmony and purposeful relationship with each other, and with all creation. *Shalom* surpasses our language to comprehend all that it embraces. But because we were made for this, it is for this that we yearn. And it is precisely this that God comes offering to us in the person of Jesus Christ. *Shalom*, then, is another way to describe such terms as *salvation, redemption, Dominion of God,* or *New Creation*. It is God's "peace which passes understanding."

Shalom is what Chip is seeking, even though he hasn't the capacity to express it. When his three friends sit across the table from him, they hear the cry of his heart. So it is with any of us when we sit over coffee with our friends who are still lost and hear their quest for something more—whether those persons across the table are winsome, such as Chip, or confrontational. Our dilemma is that we want with all of our hearts to communicate God's good news to them. Yet we meet a complex set of problems. Immediately we realize that when humankind (confronting us in our friends) leaves God out of the equation, *they have no category* with which to even begin to conceive what we are trying to communicate.

This becomes more obvious, not to mention more confusing, for Chip's postmodern generation for whom (to borrow from Gertrude Stein) *there is no there, there!* Ambiguity is an acceptable way of life for these friends. The very notion of there being *the way* to God is highly suspect. Their irreverent and confused and eclectic quest after "spirituality" floats free from any exclusive commitment. We are looking at a culture that accepts many truths, all equally valid, and cannot make sense of an exclusive claim of Jesus as Truth. A culture that invents and designs its own gods and allows for the legitimacy of multiple *selves* is not congenial to the unique claim of Christ as being the only way to God. And yet that is precisely our message.

Impossible task? Yes! It always has been. We must be very sensitive to the realities we face. Sincere intentions will not suffice. We are reminded again of the words of an Indian evangelist who said: "He who has not prayed has not even begun the work of evangelism."[1] In our love for those whom we confront in their *lostness,* we are driven not only to prayer, but to an honest appraisal of our own understanding of the complexity of these friends.

THE LAUGHINGLY IMPOSSIBLE TASK

We know that we are mandated to be faithful witnesses to what we have seen and known and experienced of God's love in Christ. But face it: We who have responded to Jesus' "Come unto me!" invitation have also *entered into* the world of the biblical narrative. We have seen and heard what human eyes and ears have not. We accept and are formed by that understanding of Jesus Christ who is *the* Truth. How this ever happened is part of the mystery we share inside the Christian community. We have entered into the realm of God's *Shalom* made possible through Jesus, the realm of the Spirit of God. It is all very real to us. At the same time it is still a lot of *fool-ishness* to Chip and to our friends who are outside. Even though Jesus is the very *Door* Chip seeks! How, then, do we equip ourselves when we are challenged with the question: *What does Jesus have to do with anything?* Here are several dimensions which deserve our response.

1. Our friends need to hear an informed understanding of not only our own experience of Christ, but of who Jesus is, what he was all about, what he did, what he taught, and how that relates to us any kind of good news. Quiet conversation, along with unhurried and sensitive time spent clarifying their "database" of Christian information, is the preferred and proven method. We who love them must be patient, sensitive, and unthreatened by their often abrupt and even hostile questions. This means that we need to have our own database well-informed from the biblical narrative.

2. Our response needs to be more than merely verbal or conceptual. These friends need to *see* what it looks like in both our *individual* and *communal* experiences. What does the gospel do? If Jesus is the Door into New Creation, then what does a *New Creation person,* or a *New Creation community* look like? How do we live out such an *alien* reality in the midst of the mucked-up and far-from-ideal realities of daily life?

3. Our friends need to know what is involved in — the implications of — *following Christ.* We dare not be religious hustlers or charlatans making false claims. We must be able to communicate convincingly not only the *promises* of God in Christ, but also the *consequences* and demands Jesus makes of those who follow him. And here is where we come to another *uncomfortable* dimension of our Christian gospel, namely that the life of the follower of Christ is a life lived in *obedience* to one Lord, which radically transforms life's priorities.

Does Jesus give new life? Yes. Forgiveness? Yes. Peace? Yes. Adoption into God's family? Yes. Hope even when there is no human hope? Yes. Meaning and abundant life? Yes. All these and more are among the extravagant promises of God. But then, there is the flip side: "If you love me, keep my commandments." "Everyone who hears these words of mine and puts them into practice is like a wise man who builds his house upon a rock." "If any persons will come after me let them deny themselves, take up their cross and follow me." "A new commandment I give you, that you love one another as I have loved you."[2] Such demands do not remotely allow us to go on comfortably and placidly living our lives and conducting our daily business apart from the mission of God. Our friends need to hear all of this from us and see it demonstrated in us.

4. The very awesome, irrational, transformational necessity of the Cross and its centrality to all that Jesus came to be and do must never be muted. Nor must it be spiritualized into something that it is not. But that is the subject for our next chapter. Here I raise the subject because of what follows in this chapter: We must communicate a fascinating message of Jesus and his teachings, all the while knowing that it culminates in the Cross.

Our friends deserve these answers from us. This also is part of the mystery of God's working in and through us (which we commonly refer to as *evangelism*). What we know is that as we, followers of Christ, live out New Creation, and demonstrate its reality in a community called the church, and articulate such all-encompassing good news of Jesus to our inquiring but unseeing friends, then God also works simultaneously in and through "the foolishness of what we preach" to open blind eyes and deaf ears and rebellious hearts to himself! We are not alone in this work of communicating the reality of Jesus Christ. Jesus calls us into the mission of God, and that mission is God's own compassionate mission for those outside. As humanly impossible as it is, the miracle is that God in Christ walks with us and in us in our obedience to himself, and so draws others to himself.

Personal and Public Dimensions of the Good News of Jesus _____

There are both *personal* and *public* dimensions to the message and the call of Jesus. The *personal* side is an inner response of mind and will to what we know and understand of Christ and his message. This response brings us into relationship with the person of Jesus Christ and to personal *Shalom*. In so responding, we enter into Christ and he enters into us. Our minds and wills are transformed by God's Spirit and progressively brought into sync with the mind and will of God in Christ. It is this personal and inner response that deals with our personal lostness and brings us hope and newness, as well as the assurance of forgiveness and acceptance with God. Through this response we find our *heart's true home*. We are reconciled to God and embraced in his love. Christ comes to live out his life in and through us. These promises of the gospel are precious and have been the focus of so much of the praises of the Christian community.

But the call to follow Christ cannot be confined to the inner self (to which the enlightenment, and modern philosophy, would relegate all religion). It has a decidedly *outward* and *public* dimension that lives and obeys the gospel visibly in the *public square* of human events as Christ lives in and through us!

This is to say that when we are talking about Jesus and the gospel, we are talking about anything but a purely subjective (or silent) faith. The gospel of Jesus is visible, controversial, often confrontative, and at times offensive. This public gospel is at the heart of what Jesus came to be and to do, especially in his teachings. In the New Testament documents, this public gospel goes under the rubric of the *gospel of the kingdom of God*.

It is this very *gospel of the kingdom of God* that too often gets reduced or truncated in many popular expressions of Christianity. The gospel of the kingdom is nothing less than a holistic world and life understanding of what Jesus came to be and do. It is the promise of the return of true *Shalom*. But because it makes such radical demands upon those who would embrace it, it is embarrassing to those who would seek to *market* the gospel or make it user-friendly to the masses seeking (humanly defined) peace and self-fulfillment.

Still, these *demands of the gospel* are very much at the heart of the message of Jesus. Here it is enough to say that Jesus is the unimaginable good news of God, and the One who inaugurates God's New Creation. In him only is God's *Shalom* both returned and brought to its perfection.

Two Interpretive Points

At this point I introduce two interpretive points that I believe to be crucial to our pursuit of understanding Jesus and the compassionate mission of God to which he calls us. Only then do I intend to move on to consider who Jesus is, what he did, and what he taught and calls us to.

Jesus the Subversive

The word *subversive* has all kinds of negative connotations. But it is not too much to call Jesus a subversive (or perhaps more accurately, a *countersubversive*). The sheer *radicalness* of who Jesus is, the sheer *otherness* of what he taught, the sheer *unexpectedness* of what he did, these continue to be far too *subversive* (and controversial) for many, if not most, who hear them for the first time (or even repeated times!). This is so simply because they are alien to the principles of the context which have formed us. Consider, however, that the rebellion against God by our human parents at the beginning of the biblical story (see chapter three) was by any definition a *subversion* of God's *Shalom*. So, conversely, the redemptive event of Jesus in human history was designed to *subvert the subversion!* There's nothing user-friendly about that!

Christians are always tempted to rewrite the script of the gospel to make it more comfortably fit our categories of the *humanly acceptable*. In so doing, we deny the wisdom and power of God that do not in any way fit these categories. We need to understand that such radical distortion, that subversive tragedy called *sin* which we discussed in the last two chapters, is going to require a radical *countersubversion*. And that's *exactly what salvation is!* If *sin* is leaving God out of the equation, and thus introducing Death into the scene, then how is God to intrude Life back into the scene so that the *equation of sin* no longer works? Or, if sin subverted the order of creation and defaced God's *Shalom*, then how is God going to *subvert the subversion* so as to inaugurate a New Creation where there is peace and joy and righteousness in the Holy Spirit? How is God to show the rebellious powers their folly? How will the Creator-God show his own rebellious and screwed-up humanity his redemptive alternative, the glory of God's New Creation that we call *salvation?* How?

Everything about Jesus is a *head-on collision* with the human community who has left God out of the equation. To a generation obsessed with a hyperactive quest for some illusive goal of self-fulfillment, or some ambiguous spirituality, Jesus comes plainly announcing that the way to find it is through self-denial: "Whoever finds his life will lose it, and whoever loses his life for my sake will find it."[3] That much for starters. To persons insisting upon their *rights,* and pursuing their autonomous quest for whatever it is that those *rights* will accomplish, Jesus can only say: "Take up your cross and follow me." To those seeking *comfortable and inoffensive religion,* Jesus offers the offense of the cross, he offers suffering, he offers himself as the Lamb of God by whose *blood* and *death* true peace is purchased!

God's plan is subversive, to say the least, of all humanly contrived authority structures, power structures, and all other human idolatries, whether political, economic, religious, or cultural. At the same time it is wonderfully realistic and compassionate. *Radically gracious.*

Jesus from the Margins

The other interpretive point which flows from the first is that Jesus arrived on the scene and operated from the very *margins of society.* The God of the biblical story has been described by someone as the God of "left-handed ways." Jesus' coming was just such. When he came as the Word of God made flesh, his coming was a total *end-run* around all human expectations of any messianic visitation. It avoided any semblance of power, splendor, grandiosity, pomp, or triumphalism. That was and is a scandal to human wisdom. Where were the armies, the universities, the corporate headquarters, the world's acclaim?

Jesus was the controversial child (his mother was a virgin) of peasant parents in an occupied nation, on the edge of the empire. The occasion of his birth was a political mandate to register for taxes by an oppressor nation, and his birth took place in a strange city without hospitality. As if this were not enough, his birth also precipitated a blood bath of genocide by a petty official (this part of the Christmas story doesn't get much attention!). Jesus' family escaped into exile and spent years as refugees in a foreign country. Upon their return, they took up the ordinary daily tasks of a working family in a small city. His itinerant ministry as an adult was primarily a rural affair.

And this was the Son of God?

Face it! Jesus and his life and teachings just *don't make sense* to our *lost* friends. Yet it is this very *doesn't-make-sense-Jesus,* this *God-from-the-margins,* this subversive Jesus and his teachings, who rescues us and who is the very door into true *Shalom.*

The fact is that this from-the-margins principle is deeply imbedded in the way God continues to work, and it continues to be an embarrassment. It is an embarrassment to a concept of the gospel that is conformed (captive?) to the plausibility structures of modern society, with its focus on wealth and power. Church history corroborates the principle. Whenever the church becomes so preoccupied with acceptance, stature, reputation, place, influence, and institutional prosperity, count on God to do another *end-run* and show forth his power and wisdom in the least acknowledged of the human community from the margins of society. The New Testament accounts do not themselves make sense apart from this pair of interpretive lenses!

We need now to look at the biblical accounts and *refound* our understanding of Jesus. While the *comfort* of the gospel may seem

Subversive Jesus, Radical Grace

quite *uncomfortable* by human standards, it inexplicably operates at the deepest and most profound levels of human experience. And, ironically, it does not mean the absence of pain and conflict in our human pilgrimage. Quite the contrary. God's *Shalom* and *comfort* are wonderfully experienced in the midst of the human tragedy with all of its pain and conflicts and inexplicable mysteries. One has only to look at the life and teachings of Jesus to see this demonstrated.

JESUS: THE TRULY HUMAN ONE

Chip's generation is not all that impressed with talk! He and his friends really want to see any answer to their issues walking and talking in flesh and blood. This abruptly brings the church back to a sometimes forgotten, but major dimension of our message. In the church's zeal to guard and honor Jesus' deity, his oneness with God the Father, too often it has muted his true humanity. And this is a travesty. Jesus is, after all, true humanity; he is the firstborn of the New Creation; he is *paradigm man.*

In the last chapter we discussed the dimensions of lostness. But what about Jesus? He was not lost. None of those descriptions apply to him. Jesus lived in the middle of very difficult social and religious crosscurrents, but with utter *Shalom.* He knew who he was. He knew where he had come from. He knew why he had come. He understood and loved his neighbors as well as all that God had made. He was not put off by the barriers and prohibitions that were destructive of life or human community. He was in incredible communication with God whom he intimately addressed as Father (or Daddy/Abba).

Jesus' humanity is a gift to us. More than that, the New Testament documents tell us that it is God's purpose and design to "conform us to the image of Jesus Christ."[4] He came to demonstrate human life as God intended it in his act of creation.

Indeed, this very human communication of God's purpose comes to our contemporaries who are chasing their endless *gospels du jour* of self-fulfillment or success. Jesus comes to those who may be seeking to cope by escaping into the narcotic of hedonism in its endless expressions. He comes to those in frustrating quests of meaning, hope, and intimacy.

It is only natural to ask the question: How did (and does) God the Creator communicate his compassionate love for people of such resistance and suspicion?

God did it in personal and truly human terms. Can we learn from that?

Jesus As Mentor

Chip's generation is almost immune to *words* and drowning in ambiguity, but nonetheless they are looking intently for a *model* they find genuine and compelling. Consider the quest for whatever true *freedom* is all about. Jesus not only was absolutely free, but he also promised that to continue in his word would make men and women his disciples, and it would make them *free indeed.*[5] So the very human Jesus models *Shalom,* and *true freedom,* and *abundant life.* Jesus is also the ultimate *Mentor.* Not only did he teach, but he invited men and women to follow him, to watch him, to ask questions, to learn from him.

Mentors are the teachers of choice to many young men and women today. A mentor is not a textbook! Mentors, first of all, *are* persons of genuineness and integrity. They are persons who have done or accomplished something commendable which demands our attention. They are available in the context of warm relationships to spend significant time with those attached to them. Jesus meets those parameters and calls upon those who follow him to become like him, to walk the talk.

Jesus as God's word of *Shalom* has come not in a disembodied state, but rather as a *model* and a *mentor* of who God is and of what true humanity is all about. Can you imagine One who is self-consciously rooted in eternity? His identity is not determined by the response of those around him or by the alien context in which he lived and walked. He had no false self-image, no false estimate of who he was, and certainly no self-delusions of any reality apart from God his Father. Jesus acknowledged the mystery of life, but his calling to be God's Son and to do the Father's will was never in question. Because of this he was also identified with the very Truth of God so that he could with integrity say that he, himself, was the Truth, and that his words were Truth and Life. No confusion there. To hear and respond to his words and his person was to respond to Truth.

Can this guy be for real?

Very Human, Yet . . .

What makes this mystery of Jesus as both God and true man so amazing is that he was not some otherworldly religious aberration. Yes, Jesus loved God with all of his heart and mind and soul and strength. But it was that love which also enabled him to love neighbors (sinners, lepers, crooks, and all) with God's redemptive love. Then, note: He could also love them as he loved himself. There is, you understand, a valid and wholesome *self-love* that is part of the *Shalom* of living in love for the Creator and the Creator's design for our neighbors. These loves are all symbiotic and each is incomplete without the others. Jesus incorporated all of the teachings of the Old Testament law and prophets as finding their true meaning in these three loves.

Mix into the mystery that Jesus experienced temptation, weakness, weariness, pain, sorrow, and even anger. All of this gave him an authenticity which attracted those on a quest in their day just as Chip and so many of those *outside* do in our own day. They saw and experienced something in him that drew them closer. Children wanted to be with him. The most rejected of society found him to be good company. That says worlds.

Jesus came to be and do much more than this, but we need to begin here as we look at how God communicated his own being and love and life and *Shalom* to us. The *word* God used to communicate his own design came as a truly human person, taking on real flesh and blood, walking and talking with other human beings in the total human experience — temptations, sufferings, weariness, and all. Keep this in mind because to accept his invitation is to invite Jesus to come into our lives and live his life in us. Or as one New Testament writer reminds us, it is the eternal purpose of God to conform us to the image of his Son!

When Jesus calls us today to *receive* him and to *abide* in him, such identity brings us into a profound understanding of our lives in the mission of God. We are accepted by God. Jesus identifies himself with us, takes up his abode in those who receive him, assures us that we are not left to our own resources. His life of worship and adoration of the Father becomes ours. We are given meaning, a hope, and a future. All of this takes away the devastating anxieties of life. And Jesus underscored this when he told his believing followers: "As the Father has sent me, even so do I send you into the world." That could bring some more-than-human exhilaration into life, couldn't it?

JESUS: INAUGURATING GOD'S NEW CREATION _____

Any candid, first-time look at the gospel accounts in the New Testament reveals that Jesus came onto the public scene with a somewhat enigmatic (to us Gentiles) but fascinating message:

> *Jesus went into Galilee, proclaiming the joyous news of God. "The time has come," he said. "The kingdom of God is near. Repent and believe this incredibly good news."* [6]

Jesus came as the messenger declaring that it was God's appointed time and that God's sovereign dominion was at the very doorstep, and this continued throughout his preaching. His message, therefore, deserves our *very* careful attention as we attempt to understand who Jesus really is and what he is all about.

It is here in this *kingdom of God* theme that the transformational and recreative work of Jesus Christ has *teeth* and brings redemptive change! It is as the church obeys Jesus' teachings of the kingdom of God that those teachings become a visible demonstration on the human stage. It needs to be reiterated that there are, in fact, several different New Testament terms which refer to this same kingdom reality, and which are nearly synonymous. In different New Testament writings we find: the *Kingdom of God, Eternal Life, New Creation, the Age to Come, Salvation, the Good News of God* (gospel), and perhaps even the New Testament usage of the word *Righteousness,* all of which speak of God's rescuing and redemptive mission in Jesus Christ. But in the first three New Testament gospels, it is the *gospel of the kingdom of God* which is the dominant theme of Jesus' message.

Jesus' word about his own return at the end of this age significantly says: "And this *gospel of the kingdom* will be preached in the whole world as a testimony to all people groups, and then the end will come."[7] This is the all-encompassing message. Jesus' own death and role as the sin-bearing Lamb of God, which are at the heart of his mission, are everywhere obvious in his conversations with his own disciples, but this is *not* the primary theme of his public preaching! Rather, it is that the sovereign dominion of God is breaking into the human scene in order to redeem and to create all things new. Jesus' roles as the Anointed One who inaugurates God's dominion and as sin-bearer on the cross are both of one piece. They are at the heart of what he came to do. Neither must be slighted or diminished.

In Luke's version of Jesus' missionary commission to his disciples, these two themes both appear as Jesus says: "Everything must be fulfilled that is written about me in the Law of Moses, the Prophets and the Psalms. . . . This is what is written: The Christ will suffer and rise from the dead on the third day, and repentance and forgiveness of sins will be preached in his name to all nations."[8] It is interesting for our purposes here that Jesus underscores the fact that the Old Testament Scriptures (the Law of Moses, the Prophets, and the Psalms) all taught who he was and what his messianic ministry included, especially the necessity of his sufferings and that his death was no accident.

But in Matthew's more familiar version of Jesus' missionary commission to his followers, he never mentions his sufferings and death. Rather, he charges them to *make disciples* in every ethnic group in the whole world. No small vision there! That task was to include not only initiation (baptism) but also teaching new disciples to observe (obey) *everything* that Jesus has taught them. And what would that be? Obviously, because we have six of Jesus' sermons recorded in Matthew (all of which give us something of a *blueprint* of what New Creation is to look like in flesh and blood), it should be apparent that this would be the thrust of their *disciple-making* ministry. The first of these is the Sermon on the Mount, recorded in Matthew 5-7. It splendidly spells out the design, or blueprint, of the community of the kingdom of God (the church). The kingdom community will be composed of persons who, by their *kingdom-shaped* lives, will thereby become the light of the world and the salt of the earth.

Antecedent Expectation

The initial proclamation about the kingdom (dominion) of God did not explode on the scene without expectation. The very idea that there was "an expected (or appropriate) time of Yahweh" had to ring a bell somewhere. Vague but hopeful ideas of a new exodus, of a deliverance from captivity, of the manifest reign of Yahweh floated around in the Jewish psyche in those post-exilic days. And that Jesus was announcing that this "time" had arrived was dramatic to the point of being presumptuous![9]

All of this anticipation flows out of the Old Testament documents (the Law and the Prophets), which were the common property of the community to which Jesus was preaching. Although some hints of such a universal reign of God appeared quite early in the Scriptures (to Abraham: "In your seed shall all the nations of the earth be blessed," and to David: "Your throne shall endure forever"), they only began to take on more substance with the Hebrew prophets around the seventh century B.C. These eccentric seers not only decried Israel's unfaithfulness to the theological and social requirements of their own Torah (which was their national covenant), but spoke of a future "day of the Lord" when "the arm of the Lord" would exercise itself to establish justice and peace within the human community.

Isaiah, in particular, spoke of one whom God would designate as "my Servant" and as an "Anointed One" (in Hebrew, *messiah,* or in Greek, *Christ[os]*) who would be "a light for the Gentiles" and "my salvation to the ends of the earth."[10] This Servant, seeing the absence of *justice,* and the indifference to such behavior, would respond with justice.[11] Into this prophecy came also the promise of the *Spirit,* by whose agency both the Servant and God's people would be empowered to effect justice and righteousness.

The anointing of the Servant was specifically to accomplish God's compassionate restoration of the human community.[12] This passage came in the same general context as another graphic revelation of God's heart and agenda, in which he rebuked his people for their superficial religion. He called them to: "loose the chains of injustice . . . to share your food with the hungry and to provide the poor wanderer with shelter—when you see the naked, to clothe him."[13]

Isaiah also spoke of the Servant's key role as sin-bearer, as the one who would suffer for us and in our place: "But he was pierced for our transgressions, he was crushed for our iniquities; the punishment that brought us peace was upon him, and by his wounds we are healed."[14]

Both of these messianic roles are fulfilled in Jesus. He is the implementer of justice and champion of the oppressed, as well as sin-bearer. Both are critical to our understanding of the gospel. Neither must be diminished one whit. We are not free to rejoice in one and ignore the other. We need to see in Isaiah's teachings the first strains, the beginning notes, of New Creation. We need to see with truly biblical eyes a whole new understanding of God's design for the human community, where justice and peace are operational.[15] However inarticulate this hope may have been in post-exilic times, it was tangible and real nonetheless. The messianic expectation was in the air.

Imagine, then, the drama of an angel announcing to a teenage virgin that the unexpected and miraculous life in her womb would sit upon the throne of his father David and that his kingdom would never end.[16] Think of the implications of Mary's response, the sheer radicalness of what she was saying, and how it echoes the very concerns of the Hebrew prophets:

> *My soul magnifies the Lord . . . he has shown the strength*
> *of his arm, he has scattered the proud in the imaginations*
> *of their hearts, he has put down the mighty from their*

thrones, and exalted those of low degree, he has filled the
hungry with good things, and the rich he has sent away
empty. He has helped his servant Israel, in remembrance
and mercy, as he spoke to our fathers, to Abraham and to
his posterity for ever.[17]

Consider the drama at the beginning of Jesus' public ministry when he entered the synagogue in his home town, read the passage from Isaiah, then forthrightly affirmed: "Today this scripture is fulfilled in your midst."[18] For the first time we see controversy. The admiration of neighbors for this local boy certainly did not include such presumptuousness as this. Nor were these expectant Israelites prepared for the demands and redefinitions which Jesus brought, especially his claim to be the only Son of the Father. The very idea of a carpenter's son having anything to do with their messianic expectation! From that point Jesus began his itinerant ministry as teacher and preacher of the kingdom of God.

What Does the Kingdom of God Look Like?

Only when we come fully to grips with what Jesus preached and taught do we begin to comprehend something of both the hostility he generated and the transformational impact which flows from those teachings when they are practiced by those who embrace him as Messiah. It is these teachings that are the most radical, subversive, and *uncomfortable* dimensions of the Christian message. The kingdom of God stands in absolute missionary confrontation with and redemptive alternative to the *chaos,* the nature of this world in its rebellion against God. Jesus redefines *everything* in all of human existence in terms of God's *Shalom*—everything! His teachings do not *fit* merely human categories.

It is strange, or perhaps tragic, that there is so much *talk* about the kingdom of God in the church, and yet so often we seem mindlessly not to ask the obvious question: What in the world does the kingdom of God (or God's New Creation) look like? What are its characteristics? What are its dimensions? What makes kingdom people to be *salt* and *light?* The answers to such questions are quite plainly before us in all of Jesus' teachings, but nowhere more so than in the twice-recorded sermon which we generally designate: the Sermon on the Mount (Matthew 5-7) and the Sermon on the Plain (Luke 6).[19] His other sermons (especially in Matthew) simply enhance what he taught in these.

The Sermon on the Mount and the Sermon on the Plain reveal the heart and mind of God and are integral to the gospel we declare. They are a digest of what the kingdom looks like in personal and communal demonstration. The Messiah, the Servant of God, came to accomplish salvation, which included bringing the return of God's *Shalom*. God's compassion for the crushed and broken and helpless, as well as his intense desire for intimacy with his creatures, is so obvious. But one has only to look at these sermons to see that true blessedness, true human fulfillment, comes in strange ways. God's *Shalom* is upon those who are either poor (Luke), or those who identify with the poor (Matthew), upon those who weep, upon those who hunger physically (Luke) and those who hunger after *righteousness* (Matthew). So also with those who show mercy, who are quite willing to be peacemakers and to suffer for the causes of justice and righteousness.[20]

This is all only comprehensible as we understand that the kingdom of God is totally *other* than what this world sees and understands. It has been described by Donald Kraybill as "The Upside-Down Kingdom," which is a most apt description.[21] As I said earlier, Jesus *redefines everything*. The *joy* Jesus offers is his own joy, which is experienced by accomplishing the Father's will, and that included a cross: "Who for the joy that was set before him endured the cross." The *peace* that Jesus offers is "not as the world offers" but comes from being at one with God in a relationship of intimacy and love. *Success,* in kingdom terms, is only in faithfulness to God's mission unto the very end, and in the midst of trials and chaos. *Wealth* is described in terms of true riches, *not* silver and gold, stocks and investments, but treasures laid up in heaven, namely faith and obedience to the teachings of Jesus. *Power* is defined in terms of weakness and servanthood, not in political coalitions and quests for the top spot, not in triumphalism, but in adherence to God's design in the midst of human weakness. *Freedom,* in kingdom living, is in being formed by Jesus' Word, by the Truth.

This is the flavor of the "upside-down kingdom." This is the blueprint of New Creation. This is what the unfaithful church and its truncated proclamation too often fails to comprehend. It is because this agenda is so *otherworldly* that Jesus would say even to a religious leader such as Nicodemus: "Unless a person be born again he cannot *see* the kingdom of God." The kingdom is always in a head-on collision with the idols of contemporary life—the idols of economic power, political power, ethnic power, social power, even ecclesiastical power to which men and women sell their souls. This is not to mention the plausibility structures of the culture that dismiss the good news of Jesus with condescension and contempt.

Jesus teaches us that our very first priority is to seek to be formed by his kingdom teachings: "Seek first the kingdom of God and all these other things shall be yours also." His commission is not to go and offer a reduced message of safety, certainty, and enjoyment; not a message of health and wealth; not "cheap grace." Rather it is to make disciples who observe "all that I have commanded you." Paul makes this even more explicit when he says that God's *predestined* purpose in calling us is to "conform us to the image of his Son."[22] This is exactly why the world *hates* Jesus and his followers, namely, because they (we) do not play by the world's rules. This is why there is included in the Sermon on the Mount the blessing on those who are insulted and persecuted, falsely spoken against with all kinds of malice.[23]

All of which is why this hugely dominant theme and its observance are so often conveniently muted or ignored, in order to make the gospel more palatable, or marketable, to fickle consumers (translated: potential church members!). It is here, above all, that the messengers of the gospel are too often guilty of *elision,*[24] or surgically slicing out Jesus' uncomfortable or embarrassing demands for a life of radical obedience to his teachings. They try to avoid conflict with, or outright rejection by, those who continue to leave God out of the equation.

No amorphous spirituality here. This is what salvation will look like in a human community amidst flesh-and-blood realities, and which outsiders can *see* and respond to in praise to God! Neither are the teachings of these sermons any kind of bland *inner religion* that leave us untransformed or indistinguishable from the lostness of those who haven't responded. The kingdom of God is rooted deeply in not only the sovereign good purpose of God to save a screwed-up creation, but also in a people who mirror his own being, character, heart, and image!

These teachings are also the clue to the meaning of Jesus' enigmatic metaphor of the small gate and the narrow road that lead to life,[25] along with the even more disturbing consequence, "and few there be that find it." It was G. K. Chesterton who observed that it is not that the gospel has been tried and found wanting, rather it has been found difficult and not tried!

If, then, we are to be faithful to the gospel which is given us by God in Jesus Christ, we must faithfully demonstrate and declare *all of it,* not just its wonderful *promises* of forgiveness and new life by the Spirit. We are called to "prove the will of God" also in the *demands* which are found in Jesus' plain teachings. The first of these demands, always at the threshold of Jesus' invitation, is the command that we should *repent.*[26] It also adds urgency to the teachings which speak of the purpose of the gospel being to bring every people-group to believe and obey him, and the sobering warning to those who do not believe and obey.[27]

This does not at all diminish God's offer of extravagant love and radical grace in any way. But it does remind us that the same free grace by which we are saved is for the purpose of producing a New Creation: "For we are God's workmanship, created in Christ Jesus to do good works, which God prepared in advance for us to do."[28] The calling of Jesus and the gospel is "out of darkness and into his wonderful light."[29]

It is also true that in our cynical, sullen, and word-weary culture, it will be the works of God's kingdom folk that will be the most effective proclamation of the gospel and will later give words their credibility. It is, as I have said, all so laughably impossible in human terms. But it is by the preaching of this foolishness, and the living of these upside-down and obedient kingdom lives, that God will accomplish his saving work in our friends still outside. It is our obedience to this gospel of the kingdom that is our visible witness to Jesus' mission to restore true *Shalom* in individual lives, in society, and in all of creation which groans in the birthing pains of God's redemption.

The Cross:
Violent Love

*How can anything so violent have anything to do
with anything good about God, or about love for his
screwed-up creation?*

—Chip

The person of Jesus as truly human, as our mentor, as the teacher of the kingdom of God, of New Creation, all seems innocent enough, even attractive. Many persons who have never come anywhere close to the Christian understanding of discipleship have admired Jesus as a good man and a great teacher. But that misses the point. The point was not lost on Chip. He had lived his life in total secularity and was altogether bewildered by one piece of his encounter with Kate and the other followers of Jesus. That had to do with the point of the Cross. In his first meeting with Kate in the Episcopal Church service, he did not comprehend what happened at the Eucharist, when the church folk went down to the front and the priest said something about the body and blood of Jesus. He did not understand then, and neither does he understand now, the symbol of the Cross which pervades so much of the Christian practice.

His innocent questions were refreshing. One that he raised early on was quite basic: "What is a *cross* anyway?" When the three friends explained to him that it was a cruel means of executing criminals in the ancient Roman world, his next question was even more probing: "How can anything so violent have anything to do with anything good about God, or about love for his screwed-up creation?" Good question. How could a person such as Jesus, who loved and served and taught, elicit such a violent and irrational hatred from those in places of influence? So why the Cross? Why so focal, so central to the whole story of Jesus, to the Christian church's tradition? To begin to respond to that enigma is the task now before us, and it is not at all neat and clean and *spiritual!*

Nowhere is the "foolishness of what we preach"[1] more clearly epitomized. To say that the Cross rewrites history, that it redefines authority (and everything else), has been the conclusion of the Christian community for two millennia. How did it ever come to such a conclusion? Chip was understandably bewildered.

The Cross is far too *irrational* for the rational, and it is far too *irreligious* for the religious. The Cross really does not conform to any human categories. It is beyond that which any human mind could ever even imagine, or even want to imagine. It is also far too radical and disruptive and subversive and controversial for sophisticated user-friendly church marketers. The Cross is an offense to *comfort-zone Christianity.*[2]

The Cross is not a random, unprovoked, or disconnected act of violence on which God and the Christian community have contrived to put the best face! It is rather the consummation of Jesus' work of love in rescuing God's creation from its chaos, from its *missing-the-point,* from its deserved destruction, from God's displeasure and holy wrath. The Cross is at the heart of restoring *Shalom.* It is the Cross that makes our participation in the kingdom of God, in God's New Creation, even possible.

But we're still begging the question. Why this violent reaction, this cruel episode of suppression? The answer comes in the very teachings of Jesus. Primarily it was his teaching that spelled out a very radical alternative to the other commonly accepted solutions

Subversive Jesus, Radical Grace

to salvation—the *gospels* of his day—which precipitated the Cross. God's dominion, as proclaimed and lived by Jesus Christ, is still a radical alternative. It creates the major problem we still have with all of the unlikeliness and foolishness of the *gospel of the kingdom of God*—namely, that it is true!

CHIP'S ISSUES GET US STARTED _____

Over the weeks, Chip kept plying his three friends with his innocent but probing questions. The whole body of what they had been talking about, right down to the violence of the Cross, consisted more of stumbling blocks than steppingstones to Chip. Three of his issues will help us:

1. His first response after hearing of Jesus and his teachings was: "Even if I could buy into Jesus as being who he says he is, the whole *God idea* makes me nervous. How would some Mr. Nice-Guy-Jesus even smile on a screwup like me? I know what I probably ought to do, but I don't want any final exam on it!" In such a comment Chip was echoing the familiar sense of anxiety over his (our) unfamiliarity with the Creator-God, and the guilt (though ill-defined) that made him more than a little uncertain about even wanting such a relationship. Would God like him and accept him? "Is God even a good deal?" (in Chip's terms).

2. His second problem with all that he had been hearing was simply honest ignorance: "So all that you guys have laid out about Jesus is okay. Interesting. Sounds like good stuff. But we're not there yet! There is a whole lot of stuff that simply doesn't compute. For instance, the Sunday I wandered into that church and met Kate, it was out of pure chance. I don't even know why I did it. And I know Christians always hang crosses everywhere, but I haven't a clue why! It may be simple to you guys, but it's a big fog area to me."

3. His third difficulty with the discussion had to do with everything outside of himself: "So what does Jesus, and the Cross, and all this stuff, even have to do with anything in our screwed-up world?"

His friends were fascinated by his inquiry. They were not at all defensive at his questions. He was tangibly curious. What he didn't know was that he was throwing down a healthy challenge to them. It is quite easy for Christian folk to become so overly familiar with the most profound concepts and the loaded words that are a part of the Christian story that they can become quite mindless about their meaning. Chip's questions were like a reality check.

The Birth of a Savior

For two millennia the church has gathered around a table or an altar—on which were bread and wine—sometimes in hushed silence, sometimes in near ecstatic song. Why? What is the significance of that puzzling experience that Chip had in Kate's Episcopal service of Eucharist?

Stand back and look at what happened between the Annunciation, when the angel Gabriel told Mary about the child she was to bear, and the Cross, where it all *appears* to come to a violent end.

When Mary learns that she is to become the mother of God's Son by the creative power of the Holy Spirit, her response is one of the most amazing statements of pure faith in the whole Bible: "I am the Lord's servant. May it be unto me as you have said." But what comes shortly thereafter is even more indicative in what it prophesies about this child's meaning. We call Mary's song of praise the "Magnificat." She exudes this hymn to her godly cousin Elizabeth, full of joy and praise to God. The words out from her mouth echo the great prophets of Israel's former days:

> *His mercy extends to those who fear him, . . .*
> *He has performed mighty deeds with his arm;*
> *he has scattered those who are*
> *proud in their inmost thoughts.*

He has brought down rulers from their thrones
but he has lifted up the humble.
He has filled the hungry with good things
but has sent the rich away empty.
He has helped his servant Israel,
remembering to be merciful to Abraham
and his descendants forever. [3]

The proud, the powerful, and the rich stand under God's judgment for contributing to the world's defilement and *chaos*. But the humble, the hungry, and the spiritual heirs of Abraham become recipients of mercy and blessings. This is quite the reverse of the ordinary sense of *haves* and *have-nots,* of wealth and poverty, of weakness and power. It has a revolutional flavor all through it. And this is Jesus' mother talking!

The Temptations of Jesus

Move ahead three decades. As Luke recounted the life of Jesus, he made a special point of saying that after Jesus had identified himself with sinful Israel by receiving John's baptism of repentance, "he was led by the Spirit" into the desert, where for forty days he was tempted by the *slanderer,* or the Devil. This clever tempter, the Devil, knowing full well who he was dealing with, sought to seduce Jesus away from his God-given path and into conformity with the acceptable human and social paths that would bring: (1) economic power, (2) popular acclaim, and (3) political power. First, he made a plausible case for Jesus securing his Davidic kingship by turning stones into bread. This act would not only feed Jesus' own hunger, but allow him to meet the economic needs of the marginal populace and thus give him great influence. Ah, wealth! To be rich and powerful had always been the seductive dream of "salvation" with humankind in its confused lostness, even though it had never produced *Shalom.* Offer the crowds economic security. Win their allegiance.

The problem with this solution is that it's a human way of salvation that leaves God out! Jesus stated the *true* truth, that what humankind really hungers for is quite other. It is a *Shalom* found only in God himself and life under God's Word. Darkened humanity tends to pander to wealth. Jesus says: "No!"

The next ploy was to provoke Jesus to accomplish his messianic role by spectacular feats of power. "Jump off the temple pinnacle! Dazzle the crowds! Show that the Scripture is fulfilled, for God will cause his angels to rescue you so that you don't get hurt." This is another false method of salvation. Garner the support of the fickle masses by some derring-do, then build an empire on that support. Jesus hurled back in the Devil's face the fact that one is to take God seriously and not seek to use him to prove one's faith. Humankind in its lostness quickly jumps onboard with whatever is popular, and marketers have a field day with that. Jesus says: "No!"

Finally, one more attempt to deflect Jesus from the path of obedience. Political power. Create a political force of incredible influence. The Devil offered a proposition: "Bow down and worship me and I'll give you all the kingdoms of the earth." Jesus later acknowledged that this Devil is "the god of this world," and so in a limited sense could fulfill this offer. This would be much less painful than a cross, and on the face of it, "a sure thing." But *Shalom* is not found in false gods, or in the Devil's alien power. Jesus knew where true power lies—in the worship of God alone. So again: "No!"

Prosperity, wealth, popularity, political power—all the false gospels of this "screwed-up" world. Jesus writes across them all: "None of the above." His light showed the emptiness of each one. How sad that so many who name the name of Jesus today don't follow him at this point.

Today Scripture Is Fulfilled

The sounds of the Old Testament prophets heralding God's true agenda, as well as his judgment upon skewed values and destructive social policies, began to ring with unmistakable clarity as Jesus returned to home synagogue at Nazareth. Fresh from his temptations, from his own personal affirmation of the redemptive path that his Father-God had assigned him—and which he had chosen—

Jesus was handed the Isaiah scroll for the reading of the day. He stood to read:

> *The Spirit of the Lord is on me, because he has anointed me*
> *to preach good news to the poor.*
> *He has sent me to proclaim freedom for the prisoners*
> *and recovery of sight for the blind, to release the oppressed,*
> *to proclaim the year of the Lord's favor.*[4]

Then he rolled up the scroll and sat down to comment on the text, which was the custom. Every eye in the room was on him as he calmly announced that this messianic prophecy about the anointing and ministry of the Servant of Yahweh had been *fulfilled* in their hearing that very day! Say what? Yes, Jesus made a clear and lucid claim to the messianic ministry. But don't rush through what that text says to get to their reaction—just yet. What is fascinating is that the anointing was to bring *Shalom* to the margins of society, to the victims of economic distress, to those in prison for unpaid debts, to those helpless because of blindness. That's the good news, the *gospel*, which Jesus was anointed to proclaim and fulfill.

The reaction? Violent!

Isaiah had also prophesied that God's people would play games with his Word, that they would come near with their mouths and lips, but that their hearts would be far from him, that their worship would be made only of rules made by men.[5] So the folk in Nazareth fulfilled that prophecy, for they didn't have ears to hear the beating heart of God in the person of Jesus. He did not fit their preconceived image, nor was his agenda theirs: "He is only a local boy. What kind of uppityness is this?" It did not matter that he was proclaiming the real good news, which had been prophesied in their own Scriptures. They had no ears for God's Dominion of Peace. So they tried to terminate him then and there.

The *kingdom* of God, the *salvation* of God, the gospel of *Shalom* were too alien for the hardened hearts of the popular religionist of Jesus' day. So he went to the margins, to the ordinary folk in their burdened lives, and offered God's thrilling news of love and hope and newness.

The Cross: Violent Love

Stir In the Acceptable Solutions to the Jewish Dilemma

To attempt to understand the violence that led to the Cross, it is necessary to know who and what were the dominant influences of the Jewish society. Several political-religious parties on the scene sought control of the Jewish destiny. All were somehow aware of the grand promises given to David from their ancient past. All were somehow aware that there was a promise given to faithful Abraham even earlier, that somehow all the nations of the earth would be blessed in him. All remembered painfully the disastrous decline and captivity of Israel several centuries before. Still fresh in their minds was the occupation of Jerusalem and the defiling of the temple under Grecian rule, along with the rebellion under the Maccabeans. Now they lived with an occupying army and a military government from the Roman Empire.

What was the solution to this shame and to life's sordid reality for them? Here's how each of these parties tried to cope. Interestingly, each group has a contemporary counterpart.

- *The Essenes.* These were the escapists: "Forsake this fallen and unholy scene and wait for God's intervention." So they built a monastery at Qumran and instituted a very disciplined life for themselves. They saw no hope apart from this isolation and discipline.
- *The Zealots.* These were the political terrorists, or guerillas, of the Jewish people. Their plan was to disrupt, to assassinate, to bring down the Roman rule by any means necessary.
- *The Pharisees.* The Pharisees were the purists, the fundamentalists if you will. They have gotten bad press. Well-meaning individuals, they knew that the judgment of God had come upon the Jews in former days because of neglect in keeping the Torah. They were determined to never let that happen again, if they could help it. So they stacked up law upon law, laws to interpret laws, until it all became oppressive.

Subversive Jesus, Radical Grace

- ▸ *The Sadducees.* The Sadducees may be likened to the official boards of a lot of contemporary churches. They had a continual "wet finger in the wind" to be sure that nothing reflected negatively on the religious establishment that might be detrimental to the economy for which they were responsible.

Add in also the ingredients of:

- ▸ *The Herodians.* These were the political opportunists who were neither fish nor fowl. The Herodian lineage of kings were not properly Jews, but Edomites. But they moved into a vacuum and made an alliance between captive Israel and the Roman Empire.
- ▸ *Priests and Levites.* The "Temple Guard," as they have sometimes been sarcastically referred to, were essentially the *clergy,* the church professionals, the ecclesiastical elite.[6]
- ▸ *Rome and Other Religions.* The Roman government was itself a religion: "Caesar is Lord!" Add to this the fact that the city of Caesarea Philippi was home of shrines to many gods even before Herod built a temple there in honor of the Emperor Augustus.[7] The acceptance of a multiplicity of religions and the outright worship of government was very much a part of the scene into which Jesus came.

None of these parties accepted Jesus. They became his continual irritants. But it was more than mutual. Jesus termed some of them "white-washed tombs" and others "a bunch of snakes." Certainly, this was not a calculated way to win friends and influence people! And it begins to explain the animosity which eventually produced violence.

It might help to understand the irrational anger if we imagined someone coming onto the U.S. scene and, for whatever reason, attaining a widespread popular following. Picture what would happen if that person were to claim an authority higher than the government and to charge:

- the Chairman of the Federal Reserve as a charlatan motivated only by greed, and captive to the interests of the rich and powerful.
- the popular clergy and television preachers as either preaching half-truths, or false gospels that have nothing to do with God's purpose in human society.
- the United States government, from the president down, as being corrupt and alien to God's design for the nation and the world.
- that the only way to have peace and order and justice is by responding to his invitation to newness.

Ridiculous? Perhaps. But such a message of judgment is not at all unlike the message that Jesus preached. He came to expose counterfeits. He judged "the prince of this world" and declared current allegiances totally false and invalid. If such were to happen today, that person would be journalistically crucified, if not worse. So you begin to see the Cross in a different light.

Shalom Demonstrated

Jesus came as Light into the religious and social and personal Darkness of Palestine. He was the living demonstration of the very newness he taught, of true hope, of God's love. He proclaimed (as we saw in the last chapter) the inbreaking reign of Yahweh. He heralded a New Creation, a salvation for which hearts yearned. But he was not just talk. There was in him an unimpeachable holiness, a transparency, a genuineness, a sensitive caring, a tangible love— all of which he explained in his preaching.

But at this point in his ministry, rejected by the leadership, Jesus resorted to parables, stories with moral truths, to convey his message: "The kingdom of God is like...," and he portrayed it as a farmer sowing seed, or a woman searching for a lost coin, or a landowner going to a far country and leaving stewards in charge. Then he lived what he taught in a life of humble servanthood, focusing his priorities on those helpless and crushed by unjust systems, or those physically afflicted, or those longing for God's reality, or those wearied by impossible burdens of life, not to mention those added by the religious leaders. Darkness and Light were now in full confrontation.

The result was an intensifying hostility, even fury, among those who inhabited the places of influence in economy, church, and state. They were all the more exercised because the common folk were responding to Jesus and not to them. Jesus turned his revealing light upon all that they stood for, and they didn't come off well at all. He quoted from their own prophets, and they were exposed as the problem and not the solution. But worst of all, Jesus actually identified himself as being one with Yahweh, with God. He even called the Holy One of Israel: "My Father."

We need to keep his sermons clearly in mind to realize how alien was his presence and teaching to their society and to ours: "Blessed are you poor, . . . woe to you rich, . . . blessed are you merciful, . . . blessed are you makers of peace *(Shalom),* . . . blessed are you who hunger and thirst after justice, . . . blessed are you who are persecuted for the sake of what is right." Even his statements about who he understood himself to be provoked the rulers, authorities, powers of this dark world, and spiritual forces of evil.

- ▸ When Jesus said "I am the Light," he exposed the darkness in human hearts and the world.
- ▸ When he said "I am the Truth," he exposed all that was false.
- ▸ When he said "I am the Way," he exposed the false paths to God, the alien allegiances, and idolatries of the day.
- ▸ When he said "I am the Life," he exposed all that was part of the Death.
- ▸ When he said "I am the Bread of Life," he exposed the false shepherds who did not feed God's hungry sheep with true food.
- ▸ When he said "I am the Water of Life," he spoke to the incredible spiritual thirst that was not being assuaged by those who were ostensibly making God's promises real to the people.

And so it goes. Every self-claim of Jesus exposed the hollowness of its opposite in the community. Everything Jesus was and taught came with such force that the falseness and hollowness of all other claims were shown for the lies they were. The hatred of the civic and religious leaders grew so intense that they forsook all justice, all principles, all scruples, all of their tradition, and collaborated across their own animosities to rid the scene of this one who was *the truly human one.* "We will not have this man to be king over us . . . we have no king but Caesar!"

Jesus was the Great Prophet of God, and prophets seldom fared well at the hands of God's disobedient and rebellious people.

Why the Cross? Because of the hostility of the Darkness to New Creation. And, please note, if we are to come after him, we also must take up the Cross and follow. He warned: "If they have hated me, they will hate you also." He taught: "If I had not come they would have had no sin, but now they have no cloak for their sin." As he exposed that which was destructive and dehumanizing and discouraging in human society, and in the systems of society, so the ministry of his followers should be the same. Life marked by the Cross is not some esoteric "spiritual" experience, as many faithful saints have found out the hard way! This is the most *uncomfortable* part of Jesus' message (which is usually left out of the trivialized gospel). This is not to make us psychotic and paranoid, but to remind us of the nature of the Dominion of God, which always elicits reaction in this warfare between the Lamb of God and the Beast, between Light and darkness.

That's the human side of the Cross. Jesus was executed as a political, social, and religious troublemaker, and he was a threat to the systems of his day. He was the quintessential *persona non grata*. But he was also the Prince of *Shalom* and that's where God's side of the Cross comes in.

That Mysterious Table
with the Bread and Wine _____

Back to Chip at the table of the Eucharist. Nowhere else is the heart of Christ's work for us so graphically displayed. It points directly to God's great rescue mission of men and women who were to have been the crown of his creation but now stand helpless in their slavery to sin and death—*lost*. The Table has deep roots in Old Testament teachings, and is fraught with thrilling mystery. But above all, the Table is God's invitation into the great Salvation (to the great feast of God) that he has accomplished for us in his well-beloved Son, Jesus.

Hints of God's sin solution come in the early pages of his dealings with the people of Israel. As God constituted Israel a holy nation, he gave to them a "tent of meeting" to be at the center of their encampments. He did this so that he, God, could meet with them. But because of the guilt and separation caused by their sinfulness, God provided a sacrificial system by which an innocent animal took the place of these flawed people. The animal became the substitute sin-bearer, and God accepted the animal's blood as a satisfaction.[8] A substitute was provided. Sin was forgiven. Reconciliation was effected, and the people could come before God in worship with a clear conscience—until they bombed out again! The system was a foretaste of what God had in mind for the ultimate rescue of his messed-up creatures (and creation).

God does not throw up his hands in disgust and discard us. Not at all. This is, after all, his creation, which he created to show forth the splendor of his being. The Creator-God is unimaginably patient and enduring with what would frustrate any of us to total despair. What God's infinite love has in mind for this separation becomes more focused several centuries later, when after multiple and escalating failures and flagrant violations of all they had been called to be, God makes a promise of the Servant, whom we discussed in the last chapter. Remember again the poignant description:

> *Who has believed our message and to whom has the arm of the LORD been revealed? He grew up before him like a tender shoot, and like a root out of dry ground. He had no beauty or majesty to attract us to him, nothing in his appearance that we should desire him. He was despised and rejected by men, a man of sorrows, and familiar with suffering. Like one from whom men hide their faces he was despised, and we esteemed*

him not. Surely he took up our infirmities and carried our sorrows, yet we considered him stricken by God, smitten by him and afflicted. But he was pierced for our transgressions, he was crushed for our iniquities; the punishment that brought us peace [Shalom] *was upon him, and by his wounds we are healed.*[9]

The Servant would become the sin-bearer! How would that happen?

We all, like sheep, have gone astray, each of us has turned to his own way; and the LORD has laid on him the iniquity of us all. . . . Yet it was the LORD's will to crush him and to cause him to suffer, and though the [Servant] makes his [soul] a guilt offering, he will see his offspring. . . . After the suffering of his soul, he will see the light of life and be satisfied; by his knowledge my righteous Servant will justify many, and he will bear their iniquities.[10]

Skip down the centuries again, and hear the angel speaking to a peasant girl in Palestine about a miraculous baby she is to bear: "You are to give him the name Jesus, because he will save his people from their sins." "And they will call him Immanuel—which means: 'God with us.'" Two names. One has to do with God who rescues, the other with God who wants to dwell among his people.[11] Again, in another setting, the messenger of God said to this girl: "Do not be afraid, Mary . . . you will be with child and give birth to a son, and you are to give him the name Jesus. He will be great and will be called the Son of the Most High. The Lord God will give him the throne of his father David, and he will reign over the house of Jacob forever; his kingdom will never end."[12]

Out in the wilderness of Palestine a few years later, Jesus' cousin John, an itinerant prophet, saw Jesus coming and shouted: "Look, the Lamb of God, who takes away the sin of the world!"[13] Remember all of those ancient sacrifices of lambs to deal with the sins of the people? John said that God had provided the true Lamb, who

Subversive Jesus, Radical Grace

wouldn't just deal with the sins of a fickle bunch of worshipers in Palestine, but those of the whole world. God was intruding his *Shalom* into the rebellious and screwed-up human scene in an utterly unexpected and incomprehensible way. And that same Eucharistic Table points to all of this.

Another note began to feed into Jesus' public ministry, mystifying even his closest followers. He started talking of his death at the hands of the leaders. He spoke of being "lifted up" like Moses lifted up the brass serpent to heal Israel's snake bites in the desert. He presented himself not only as the Great Prophet of God, but as the Great Priest:

> *The reason my Father loves me is that I lay down my life—only to take it up again. No one takes it from me, but I lay it down of my own accord. I have authority to lay it down and authority to take it up again. This command I received from my Father.*[14]

Or as a later writer would interpret this (my paraphrase):

> *God made Jesus to be the sin offering for us, Jesus who knew no sin, that in him we might become the righteousness of God.*[15]

Jesus also said:

> *For God so loved the world that he gave his one and only Son, that whoever believes in him shall not perish but have eternal life. For God did not send his Son into the world to condemn the world, but to save the world through him.*[16]

These statements did not make sense to his closest disciples at the time, because they were only humanly looking at a remarkable mentor and teacher. They liked being with him. They knew he was a miracle worker. They knew he was a prophet. They were optimistic that this new movement would somehow, perhaps, restore Israel to its Davidic splendor. But this *death talk* didn't compute. The idea of him being a sin-bearer was quite beyond them. Only after his death and resurrection did Jesus meet with them and interpret for them that:

> *Everything must be fulfilled that is written about me in the Law of Moses, the Prophets and the Psalms. . . . This is what is written: The Christ will suffer and rise from the dead on the third day, and repentance and forgiveness of sins will be preached in his name to all nations.*[17]

This was after Jesus had been publicly executed as a criminal in a quickly arranged trial by the religious leaders in collaboration with the Roman government. It was a travesty in every way, a good and just person being sentenced on trumped-up charges.

A "Deeper Magic" at Work on the Cross

But look at what was happening here! All of humanity's rebellion and hostility against God, all of the vaunted attempts at autonomy and power, were present at the Cross. Here were the emissaries of the Roman Empire, the priestly leaders of the nation of Israel, the prominent parties within the Israelite community (Sadducees, Pharisees, Priests, Levites, and radical Zealots) making cause together against this unlikely figure. These false authorities, who left God out of the equation and were part of the cosmic screwup, designed to get rid of this one who didn't play by their rules.

One more controversial figure put to death on the edge of the empire? That's what it would seem. But there was a *deeper magic* at work.[18] As Paul later wrote:

> *On that cross he discarded the cosmic powers and authorities like a garment; he made a public spectacle of them and led them as captives in his triumphal procession.*[19]

What Jesus did on the Cross was to redefine power and authority. He reclaimed true power and true authority for God alone. He established the Dominion of God as the only viable and forever reality. No pretenders or usurpers have any more credibility. Not Rome nor Wall Street nor the United States nor idolatrous church institutions that miss the point! The wrath of humankind against the Creator was focused on Jesus on the Cross. "We will not have this man to be king over us" they yelled (saying much more than they knew).

Those authority figures and popular crowds in their frenzy thought they had triumphed. What they did not anticipate was that, as Jesus had predicted, he would rise from the dead on the third day, and so expose their whole destructive enterprise.

Defeat Is Ultimate Victory

At the very same time that all of humanity's unjust wrath against God was executing him, Jesus was also absorbing into himself God's just wrath against all the destructive human sin, the *chaos,* and the guilt thereof. He experienced the full wages of sin, which is death. He became the sin-bearer, the Lamb of God who takes away the sin of the world. All of the tragic consequences of the *chaos* were borne by Jesus. Jesus himself is both the Great High Priest and the ultimate sin offering at one and the same time! He experienced hell for us. He was forsaken by God. He experienced the excruciating hopelessness of the ultimate dark night of existence. "God was in Christ, reconciling the world to himself" so that humankind can again have *hope.* Jesus broke the power of sin. He made *peace* by the blood of his Cross. He becomes the *Restorer of Shalom.*

How do we comprehend such a wonderful truth? We don't! We stand in awe.

All of this by way of necessary background, but Chip's question cries out to be answered in some less academic, more poetic manner to which he can relate. After all, there are untold volumes of wonderful theological scholarship trying to plumb the depths of the Cross. How to express the unimaginable?

The Cross:
"How Wide and High and Deep Is God's Love"

So profound the Cross, the implications and effect so far-reaching, that the longer one looks at it and ponders it, the larger and more all-encompassing and transformational it becomes.

- Consider all that has resulted from humankind's attempt to "be as god," to displace God in God's own creation, to attempt life and social order with merely human means and the brute selfishness of human autonomy.
- Consider the alien power of darkness, the malignant personality who sought to usurp God's ultimacy, and so is "the god of this world" whose enslaving presence inhabits our *chaos* (however you explain the Devil).
- Consider God's righteous and just wrath at such defilement and rebellion of that which he has created as an expression of his own glorious being. And consider what this rebellion has produced by way of true guilt and estrangement (even fear) that causes folk to attempt to hide from God.
- Consider what meaninglessness and hopelessness result in the human heart when the very one by whom and for whom they are created to know and love is hidden by their ignorance, stupidity, disobedience, or arrogant attempts at self-sufficiency. Consider the haunting *lostness* of not knowing who one is, or why one exists, or what it all means, or where this path leads.
- Consider that the whole of creation, as well as the human community, is thus defiled, misused, and exploited because true *Shalom* has been obscured by the cosmic *death* that has come upon it.[20]
- Consider all the humanly and socially contrived idols, solutions, power structures, ideologies, and orders which have vainly and deceptively (and, too frequently, destructively) foisted themselves off as the means of *Shalom,* and have proven counterfeit.
- Then consider the Creator-God who loves this screwed-up, guilty, lost, wayward, self-destructive creation. Consider God whose merciful heart beats with compassion like a father or mother grieving over a prodigal child. Together in the person of this God are all the elements of perfect justice, mercy, and love, and God's sovereign good purpose for it all.

What is God's answer? God's answer is the greatest and most unimaginable gift: The Cross! The Cross! The Cross!

- ▸ Consider that God comes himself in the flesh and blood of Jesus, his only Son.
- ▸ Consider that Jesus exposes the disaster of all attempts to structure life apart from the Word of the Creator, and so inaugurates the Dominion of *Shalom* . . . then makes true peace between heaven and earth by the blood of his Cross.
- ▸ Consider that Jesus, on the one hand, is the victim of all human hostility and violence against God and God's Word. Humankind seeks to rid itself of a God not of their choosing and invention. On the other hand, Jesus becomes *sin;* in his person he becomes the sin-offering and so receives God's judgment against humankind's sin, the judgment of death. In so doing, he satisfies God's justice and takes away God's wrath.
- ▸ Consider that as both fully God and fully human, Jesus is fully qualified to be the mediator between God and humankind. As both perfect High Priest and Perfect Sacrifice, he opens the way for men and women to come to God, and for the holy God to dwell among his cleansed, forgiven, and reconciled people. *Shalom!*

The Resurrection and the New World Order

But now, consider that the Cross can never be understood apart from the *Resurrection.* The Resurrection is God's affirmation that all his Son had said and done was accepted, and that he now becomes the heir of all God's creation. Jesus is alive and on the move in the world. The Resurrection was the death of death. Jesus is sovereign Lord. His everlasting dominion of *Shalom* is inaugurated with power. The sacrifice for sin was accepted, and heaven and earth are reconciled. The "all things new" begins to take shape. The age to come is now present. The Cross, inexplicable as it is, is God's word of hope, of meaning, of forgiveness, of peace, as well as the Door into New Creation. The world is now enchanted again, somehow . . . Someone is present and mysterious, Someone who sees and hears.

So the Eucharist, the table which mystified Chip, points to the mystery of the Cross:

My body, for you. My blood of the new covenant, shed for many for the cancellation of all the screwups. Do this when you are together to remember what it is all about. . . . Because you receive me, you become one with me in all that I came to be and do. As I suffered violence at the hands of those who are still part of the dominion of death, so may you. But rejoice, because my dominion is the dominion of Shalom, and it is forever, and I am with you to fill you with my joy.

The Eucharist points to the infinite joy and freedom and eternal life that is made possible by the Cross, by that very act of *violent love*. God's *radical grace* is nowhere more visible.

And because of the Cross, for these two millennia, God's people (would you believe?) actually sing about that act of violent love, about the Cross! They have, through much tribulation and misunderstanding and death, participated in the work of New Creation. But they sing because the Cross has created a new song, has made it all true and real.

This is my Father's world, O let me ne'er forget
That though the wrong seems oft so strong,
God is the Ruler yet.
This is my Father's world: The battle is not done;
Jesus who died shall be satisfied, and earth and heaven be one.[21]

That's as close as I can come to saying what is *unimaginable*. Jesus, in his love that is wider and higher and deeper than the human mind can comprehend, by his Cross, sets us free to *be* what we were created to be, to be his New Creation. But to embrace Christ by faith, to be his follower, also means embracing the agenda, the mandates, of New Creation, and the offense thereof.

It means dying to the dominion of darkness with all that it represents. Taking up the Cross is not, therefore, an empty act of devotion, but rather a way of life.

If we know this, and if this is God's word of hope to us, then the next question is: What do we do with it?

Conversion into New Creation

I feel like some kind of humanoid, functioning efficiently, but with something major missing that keeps me from being fully human. And I don't know what it is.

—Chip

"Yes and no!" was Chip's response to the question from Jong as to whether he was ready to take a step closer to Jesus. "I'm satisfied with myself . . . and dissatisfied with myself."

"I'm attracted to Jesus and scared of Jesus."

"I'm cynical about everything . . . but I want to have hope."

"I like the way I have it . . . and I'm sick of it at the same time."

"I know I ought to do a lot of things, but then again I don't really want to."

"I see something in you guys, and hear something from you, something that sounds fascinating. But honestly I don't see what you see or hear what you hear in all this thing about Jesus. I'm one of the screwups who has a hard time getting his own act together. So I'm not sure what to say to your question, or what to do with it, or even sure that I want to do anything. Does that make any sense at all?"

THE MYSTERY OF GOD'S CALLING _____

Such a response from Chip raises the fascinating question of how it is that God actually *calls* men and women into New Creation, into his *Shalom,* which is found in Jesus Christ. At one level, we are watching God work through Chip's three friends as they share with him not only stories of their own encounter with Jesus, but also their understanding of Jesus from Scriptures. At another level we're asking: What has created the dissatisfaction, the hungering for something else, the longing for the missing piece in a person such as Chip? And here we stand face-to-face with the mystery of God's working, God's calling. In some persons this calling appears to be quite abrupt and sudden. In others it may involve a long, circuitous, even agonizing process. The pursuing love of God surpasses our understanding!

What we know is that before any human "instrument" ever comes on the scene, God is at work creating such longings, dissatisfactions, and openness to even hear the claims of the message of Jesus Christ.[1] What we know is that deaf ears have to be opened, made responsive to the Spirit. And that blind eyes need to be given spiritual sight, enabled to see God's Door. What becomes obvious in the long history of the mission of God in the world is that he is not confined to merely human instruments. There are accounts of tribal traditions that prepare the way and of persons having dreams about the message before the messengers of Jesus ever appear. Sometimes miraculous events shock folk into openness to such an "unacceptable" message. This reality ought to keep followers of Jesus always praying to the God-who-calls, that he will work in the lives of those still outside with whom they will meet and communicate the good news.

At the same time, the calling is not just to "safety, certainty, and enjoyment"[2] through Jesus Christ, though such are fruits of faith. But the question also must come: A *calling* to what? The answer is a calling that includes not only forgiveness and acceptance by God, not only hope and joy, not only meaning and purpose, not only freedom and radical newness, but also *obedience* to Jesus, even *suffering* for the sake of what is right. It certainly involves a radical *change* of focus, of thinking and behavior.

The calling is always personal. God calls us through the person of Jesus. But God also calls us as persons, calls us by name: "Come unto me." Jesus is God's assurance that God loves us more than we can imagine, and we communicate that love of God to those still looking for that reality.

DARKNESS TO LIGHT

Here stands our friend Chip on the boundary between unbelief and belief (though for him it is not all that clear). He stands in the *dominion of darkness*. He is captive to its chaos. At the moment he really can't *see* what his friends see because he is spiritually blind! "The god of this age has blinded the minds of unbelievers, so that they cannot see the light of the gospel of the glory of Christ, who is the image of God."[3] But he has been introduced to the information about Jesus, and of another *Dominion*, through his friends. And according to these three friends, Jesus is the only Door into a whole new way of being, seeing, thinking, and behaving. Jesus also professes to be one with God, God's Son! According to their conversation (the church's testimony) with Chip, it is in this Jesus that one finds the key to true *Shalom*, to the "heart's true home." We are confronted, then, in such a moment as this, to the mystery of the gospel in which God is at work in the hidden depths of another person doing what human persuasion cannot do.

To our friends who are still outside the Door, still in their unbelief, it is all so unreal. How is one, then, to be set free or delivered out of such a familiar, captivating, and empty *dominion of darkness?* How is one to be delivered into that freeing *Dominion of God* with which he or she is being presented? We who have had our eyes opened can only obey Jesus and extend his invitation to these friends. *We* do not convert! We are only witnesses, ambassadors, instruments of the good news. We can invite them to "Come and see!" But the rest is up to God.

I am sending you to them to open their eyes and turn them
from darkness to light, and from the power of Satan to

God, so that they may receive forgiveness of sins and a place
among those who are sanctified by faith in me.[4]
Over all the world this gospel is producing fruit and
growing, just as it has been doing among you since the day
you heard it and understood God's grace in all its
truth. . . . For he has rescued us from the dominion of dark-
ness and brought us into the kingdom of the Son he loves,
in whom we have redemption, the forgiveness of sins.[5]

Like Kate, Barbara, and Jong did with Chip, we point men and women to the Door, who is Jesus Christ! We are living demonstrations that in Jesus we have found *Shalom,* that we have found *our heart's true home.* This is what someone did for us, and what the church has always done. We stand in the presence of God's infinite love that is calling men and women to find their true rest in him. What is more, God uses us in that ministry of calling. We stand in the presence of the *mystery* of it all, and the *mystery* of the evangelistic task given us on behalf of our friends and associates. We can only be faithful, and patient, and believing.

COUNTERFEITS THAT CAN KEEP US FROM CHRIST ____

Within the intimacy of their friendship and conversation, Chip's three friends admitted their own stories of how it was that their very *religiousness* had blinded them to their need to know Jesus as the only Door.

The trap into which Kate had fallen was assuming that her Episcopal pedigree and heritage was all that was needed. She had been baptized in infancy as a social rite in the church more than anything else. Her family and friends within the church assured her that was all she needed. Jesus Christ himself was never all that much of a factor in her experience. She had never heeded Jesus' invitation into discipleship, had never really been confronted with it. It was all a matter of external and proper religion.[6] It was familiar and pleasant, but unreal. It was only as a high school student that anyone ever showed her from the gospel accounts that Jesus wants to be asked into our lives as a living person, to be believed and *received*. That was the moment of truth when it all became real and life-changing for her.

Barbara had been turned off as a youth by the consuming busyness of religious people in her church. She assumed that the way one gained God's acceptance was to engage in all of the endless church stuff, and to be present at every church event. Her perception obscured what it was that Jesus really wants to do in lives, and it became a stumbling block. As an adult Barbara discovered that church activities are not what makes it real. It is "not because of righteous things we had done, but according to his mercy"[7] that Jesus rescues us. Barbara had briefly rebelled because she knew she could not measure up to the requirements or expectations of so many religious people. She almost chucked the whole thing until she realized that Jesus wants to set us free, not burden us.

Jong's stumbling block was different. His perception was that having the proper beliefs distinguished true Christians because the Korean church in which he grew up so emphasized that fact. He was, on one hand, incredibly thankful for the emphasis on truth. At the same time, he found a false confidence in this. He was the "darling" of his church because he was bright and well-read in the Scriptures. He could give answers to all of their questions. It was only later that he found freedom in giving Jesus full access to his life. This did not negate the concern for truth, but it set him free from trusting in his orthodox profession rather than in Christ.

These three *traps*—the trust in religious heritage, the faith in orthodox profession, and confidence in one's good works—are quite common inside the religious community, but they can keep us from Christ. Only after finding Christ as the Door do we come to appreciate the blessing of the church's tradition and community, or the blessing of the church's emphasis on Truth, or the ministry of works and obedience that flow out of lives touched by God's grace. Most of us who have grown up in the Christian community have been affected in some way or another by these pitfalls, or counterfeits. It is when we discover the wonder of Jesus Christ and invite him into our lives, when we are seriously and profoundly converted to *him* as a Person, that the joy and freedom become real!

What we have learned is the absolute truth of Jesus' words: "Apart from me you can do nothing."[8]

SUBVERSIVE GOSPEL, RADICAL GRACE: BACK TO THE BEGINNING

But here is our Chip standing *outside*, conversing with his three friends who have already gone through the Door. He is looking, longing, filled with misgivings and even cynicism, voicing his confusion. "Where does a guy even begin? How do I even begin to begin?"

"Chip," Jong explained, "we do have to respond . . . it's something like this. It's like Jesus saying to us, to you: *That's right, you can't come into my Newness on your own. That's the problem. I know that. It's not the good guys I came to rescue and make new, but the screwups. So I've covered all the guilt, removed the barriers by my Cross, and laid out the 'Welcome Mat' into my Father-God's family. I'm inviting you to trust me, that I can do for you what you cannot do for yourself, that I can make you part of my* Shalom, *my New Creation. So here's where you begin:*

- ▸ Follow me!
- ▸ I am the only Door into True Life, into the family of my Father-God. So first, with heart and mind, you have to enter, to believe that about me, and that I can do what I say.[9]
- ▸ At the threshold of my New Creation, however, is your acknowledgment of the cosmic screwup that has brought about all the chaos in the first place; in other words, leaving God out of the equation. This involves not only the chaos in your personal life, but in relationships, in society, in the environment, in all of creation. But personally it means acknowledging that the life-house (your life) which you are inhabiting is both hopeless and hopelessly condemned apart from my rescue. And then it means deliberately forsaking and renouncing that way of life, that dominion of darkness, so that you can then come and take up a new residence in me. That is where hope begins. Let me have the

title to your life, your body-residence, and give me the right to move in by my own Spirit and to make it New, as the Master Architect-Builder that I am. This is an act of your mind and of your will.

▸ When you do that, Chip, I will move into your life as both a refining Spirit, and a life-giving Breath, and my Word will begin to form you new. I will point out all of the rotten stuff and replace it. I will show you what is good and begin to install it. So I will begin the painful, but ultimately joyous and freeing, recreation of your life so that it will be intimately one with mine in the Father's plan for all of his creation. This is my radical grace at work in your New Creation.[10]

▸ When you do this, it may not seem at all dramatic because you will be in the same place, with the same people, and the same hassles. But, whereas others will still see life in only three dimensions, you will begin to see it in dimensions which you never could have imagined, and these will clarify and interpret all the rest. This is the work of my living Spirit who will indwell you.

▸ Instead of frantically and frustratingly seeking some way to be fulfilled or successful, you will find that what really gives you life is simply focusing on me, on my New Creation, on my purpose in you and your life in the world. Everything else will fall into place.

▸ Chip, this is not all on your back. When you give me entrance and rights (and sometimes you may even wonder why you did it!), then I am the one at work in you. But this is my radical grace at work. The ongoing discipline for you will be not to be seduced or brainwashed again by the "old" that you have renounced: the chaos, the screwed-up systems that you have left.

Something like that!
Let's explore all of this further.

Jesus' invitation is very simple: "Follow me!" But to follow this Person is to enter a *whole new way of life*, a new life which only he makes possible. It is on the basis of what Jesus taught, and what he did in offering himself on the Cross, that he summons us. When we do follow, we forsake our autonomy and any right to self-fulfillment. Rather, we follow Jesus into his whole new set of priorities: "Seek first the Dominion of God and his righteousness/justice, and everything else will fall into place."[11] But the beginning place is simply: "Follow me!"

Here is where we are confronted with a Door, a very personal Door. "I am the Door," Jesus said. We know that if we accept Jesus' summons that we are thereby accepting another Person to be the determinative reality in our lives. We don't know where it (he) will lead, or what lies on the other side of that Door, only that the one who invites us is the same one who has spelled out such *(subversive) joyous good news* in his teaching and preaching. He has also assured us that he is the one who can provide us with the *radical grace* necessary to make it real. And he is the one who has demonstrated unimaginable love for us on the Cross. It is he alone who is able to deliver us without blemish into the Father's family.[12]

A summons to *follow*. A command to *repent*. A decision to be made in *faith* that Jesus is the Door into New Creation, into *Shalom*.

What is even more encouraging is that there is nothing about us, no matter how private or sordid or hidden or shameful or questionable, that God does not already know—and still he invites us! His love is such that he wants us to find our *Shalom* in his presence. And he wants to recreate us to be living demonstrations of that same *Shalom!* After all, we are his creatures, and so are his by right! God's purpose in Christ is to make us participants in his own design to create all things new! It is because we are persons who are important to our Creator-God that Jesus continually summons us: "Come unto me."

But to come means walking through the Door (who is Christ), and over a threshold which involves a command to *repent* and to *believe*.[13] We need to take time to deal seriously with these two dimensions. It is not really a debate over which comes first, repentance or faith. They are intimately and mutually related to each other. One without the other is incomplete. Both are required for New Creation.

THE LIFE OF FAITH

In the life of faith we are called to the Person, Jesus Christ. He is the one who becomes the center of our focus. In coming to him we essentially acknowledge that God is again the primary reality in the equation for us. This means that we, then, come to know Jesus as he is made known to us in the writings of the New Testament. We want to learn who he is, what he did for us in his life and death and resurrection. We want to grow in our understanding of how he thinks, what he purposes, how his heart beats. It is a *life in relationship*. Think here of Jesus' use of the residential metaphor: "If you make your residence in me, and my words make their residence in you."[14] It is not at all a sterile relationship. Rather, it is an intimate one. It brings the fullness of life. But like any relationship, it must be pursued. We grow into understanding of what it means to have Jesus live in us and for us to live in him.

There is a goal in this life of faith. It is God's eternal purpose, and that for which he calls us, "to conform us to the likeness of his Son."[15] In other places this *image of God* reference is given some definition as being like Jesus in "true righteousness and holiness."[16] And again: "in knowledge in the image of [the] Creator."[17] This is pretty amazing. God doesn't call us to the life of faith to leave us formed by all the stuff of this present *chaos*. Rather out of our lives there emerges a New Creation. We begin to behave toward our neighbors as Jesus did (righteousness), and to be in harmony with the Father as Jesus was (holiness). More than that, we begin to think like Jesus did (knowledge), and Jesus thought the thoughts of his Father, the Creator.

The life of faith grows into that.

The Discipline of the Word of God in the Life of Faith

Paul, who was obeying Christ's command to "make disciples," lets us in on his own motivation for such a ministry: "My dear children, for whom I am again in the pains of childbirth *until Christ be formed in you.*"[18] In calling us to follow him, Jesus is calling us into the disciplines of New Creation, and he himself is the active agent in making all of this happen. Still he always calls us to respond with mind and heart. This life of faith is one of *mystical union* (as the church has termed it) with Jesus Christ. This calling by Jesus to "learn of me" is what also summons us to the serious and reflective study of the biblical documents. We want to learn everything we can about God, about God's inner self, about how he thinks and works. We want to know what offends God, and how God responds to our foibles and weaknesses. We want to learn of the character and mission of God. We see all of this demonstrated in flesh and blood in the person of Jesus.

A result of this immersion in the biblical documents is a wonderful promise: *freedom!* To come into harmony with the heart of God as made known in Jesus, is to simultaneously be set free from the tyranny of the *chaos,* of the dominion of darkness. Jesus' words to us are: "If you hold to my teaching, you are really my disciples. Then you will know the truth, and the truth will set you free."[19] The life of faith is a life of growing freedom, even in the midst of the most complex and intractable human circumstances. Jesus is not surprised by any life situation we're involved in, but rather is involved in it with us. The liberating teachings of Jesus equip us for this walk of faith.

In a very profound sense, our conversion is from the haunting silences of life without God and without any word from God, to a living Word from God that shatters the empty silence with hilarious songs of joy and divine love.

The Gift of the Spirit in the Life of Faith

The Word is not just an intellectual discipline. The promised (and given)[20] Spirit of the Father and the Son is the dynamic agent who works in and through this Word to form us into a New Creation. Jesus did not leave us at the mercy of our merely human resources, but after his ascension sent his own Spirit to indwell the

Subversive Jesus, Radical Grace

church, to empower it, to work creatively in and through it. The gift of the Spirit is very much at the heart of our great good news! The Spirit of Jesus living in us is very much the dynamic presence of radical grace.

The gift of the Spirit is part of our gospel, and it speaks directly to Chip's lament about his inability to even know how to respond.

We dare not in any way underestimate the necessity of God's Spirit in the work of New Creation, whether it is in us individually as part of New Creation or in the church as the community of New Creation. In one of the apostolic prayers, Paul spoke of the same Spirit that raised Christ from the dead being at work in our mortal bodies.[21] That means that all of our cop-outs and lame excuses simply don't work. God knows our human frailty. So it was that Jesus told his disciples that he would not leave them as orphans, or without another divine advocate. His enigmatic words to them were that he would come and dwell in them and that the Father would come and indwell them.[22] Mortal men and women inhabited by the Eternal God! So said the apostle:

> *Now to him who is able to do immeasurably more than all*
> *we ask or imagine, according to* his power that is at work
> within us, *to him be glory in the church and in Christ Jesus*
> *throughout all generations, for ever and ever! Amen.*[23]

The Creator Spirit is agent of this work of New Creation. In another setting the apostle spoke of the ministry of the Spirit being *glorious.* God is intentionally at work to demonstrate his own character and will in the lives of his people:

> *Now the Lord is the Spirit, and where the Spirit of the*
> *Lord is, there is freedom. And we, who with unveiled faces*
> *all reflect the Lord's glory, are being transformed into his*
> *likeness with ever-increasing glory, which comes from the*
> *Lord, who is the Spirit.*[24]

Such is the life of faith when Word and Spirit engage with our human spirits in this recreating work. When we invite Jesus into our lives by faith, then the Spirit of God invades our lives and things happen! We are being converted from our chaotic lives having only our merely human resources with which to cope . . . to men and women being dynamically empowered to newness by God's own Spirit.

The Discipline of Prayer in the Life of Faith

What we see and learn and understand of this relationship of intimacy also gives us perspective and motivation in the discipline of *prayer*. In prayer we communicate (commune) with God through Jesus Christ: "And I will do whatever you ask in my name, so that the Son may bring glory to the Father. You may ask me for anything in my name, and I will do it."[25] Such a promise from such a Person calls us deeper into the life of faith, deeper into the intimacy, deeper into the mystery of what God is doing in us and the world.

In prayer we are invited to enter into God's secret place (*worship*), and to process our lives in the light of who God is (*adoration*) and of what he has called us to be and do. Prayer can be refreshing at one time and fatiguing at another. It is in prayer that we engage this life in the presence of the two dominions (*intercession*). It is prayer that often sets us at serious odds with the community around us. We know that God invites us into his embrace as children, and that he listens very carefully even to our stumbling, sometimes stupid, complaints as well as songs of love and praise. Prayer is very much a discipline of the life of faith. It is a discipline that is learned in the doing of it.

This discipline of prayer in the life of faith takes on much larger importance as it is practiced in the community of faith (our next chapter). There are promises made to those agreeing together in prayer, as they grow and struggle together to be faithful and obedient. Our conversion, then, is also from the loneliness of isolation of broken human relationships and into a community of prayer that is in communion both with each other and with God.

Subversive Jesus, Radical Grace

THE LIFE OF REPENTANCE

Unmistakably present, however, at the threshold of this door of faith in Christ, is also the command to *repent!* [26] It gets serious at this point. The very subversive character of God's intruding his Dominion of Righteousness into the dominion of darkness has radical and transformational implications. To embrace Christ, or to be embraced by Christ, is to renounce all that made it necessary for him to be sent into the world by the Father-God and die on the cross. It is not at all a call into some spiritual self-fulfillment cult nor is it an offer to accept the blessings of God apart from the agenda of New Creation.

The person whose eyes are opened to Jesus as the Door into God's *Shalom* must not be deluded into thinking that this New Life is lived out in blissfully nonconflicted circumstances, in some spiritual *never-never-land.* One does in fact become a citizen of another Dominion, of God's kingdom, at the same time continuing to live in the midst of the same *dominion of darkness,* only now as an alien and pilgrim in the midst of that which was formerly so natural and familiar.

The New Testament documents use metaphors such as "put off the old, . . . put on the new," or "die to sin, . . . live unto righteousness," in an attempt to show the dynamic repentance that is necessary for our growth into newness. This is nowhere more graphic than in Paul's letter to the Romans. Evidently there was an early aberration surfacing there in which folk assumed that because the grace of God was so radical, it didn't really matter much if they went on indulging themselves in the patterns of the life they had formerly lived. As a matter of fact, they assumed that the more they sinned, the more God's grace would come to bear. Wasn't that wonderful? They could irresponsibly indulge their *chaotic* instincts and God would be glorified in forgiving them.

Say what?

Paul countered with a vehemence that is almost tangible.

> *By no means! Don't even talk that way! In Christ we died to sin; how can we live in it any longer? Or don't you know*

that those of us who were baptized into Christ Jesus were
baptized into his death? . . . In the same way count yourself
dead to sin, but alive to God in Christ Jesus. . . . Do not
offer the parts of your body to sin as instruments of wicked-
ness, but offer yourself to God as those who have been
brought from death to life and offer the parts of your body
as instruments of righteousness.[27]

He played out the duality of sin on the one hand, and righteousness on the other. He reminded them over and over that they
had once been slaves of sin, but now through Christ and their baptism they had become slaves of righteousness, of *Shalom*, if you
will. They had been delivered from *chaos* in order to be the practitioners of New Creation, and this involved the daily choices they
made, even the use of their physical bodies!

All of this has a price tag!

The Dominion of God is an "upside-down" Dominion. The
ancient baptismal formula was quite graphic about this. It asked
the candidate for baptism: "Do you renounce Satan and all the
spiritual forces of wickedness that rebel against God? Do you
renounce the evil powers of this world which corrupt and destroy
the creatures of God? Do you renounce all sinful desires that draw
you from the love of God? Do you turn to Jesus Christ and accept
him as your Savior? Do you put your whole trust in his grace and
love? Do you promise to follow and obey him as your Lord?"[28]

We step over this threshold of repentance into the promises of
God that are appropriated by faith. There are very practical consequences to such a step. We renounce the ways of this age and this
world to become a participant in the freedom, the joy, the *Shalom*,
the abundant life of the age to come, all of which are inaugurated
in Jesus Christ. This commits us to lives of servanthood in the cause
of loving neighbors. Such love has implications of justice, or sharing (redistribution of wealth and skills), and of the stewardship of
creation written all over it.

We live between the ages. We are continually called upon to discern between the philosophies and the dominant social orders of

this present age, and that *age to come* which is now dynamically present in the Dominion of God. We are therefore continually *dying* to one way of life, and *rising* to and *living* in another. But this means that nothing is outside the scope of Christ's calling of us into his New Creation. We respond to the demands of the gospel, and to the commands given by our Lord Jesus Christ, because we know they lead us to true life.

Discerning the Darkness in the Life of Repentance

The reality of these two dominions, of the seductions of cultural and traditional idols, of the ongoing clash between the darkness and the Light, presents New Creation folk with *a dilemma* that has no easy solution. On one hand, the community of faith trusts in God as their strong abode and sure defense. But on the other hand, while it is comforting to sing and be reminded of such when gathered with the community in worship, it is the "Monday morning world" that continually presents us with dilemmas that are complex, intractable, and never ending. These moral and ethical *shades of gray* can at times be perplexing, vexing, and eroding. How to discern the darkness? How to charitably and faithfully live as a child of the Light?

God's people have found all kinds of ways to cope with their role as "aliens and strangers in the world."[29] Some have withdrawn into monastic communities where they could live simply, engage in prayer and worship, and minister hospitality and human services to those who came to them. Others have erected strict barriers of community and tradition to protect themselves from the seductive influences of the fallen world. These communities have engaged in rigorous inner life, and often in a radical discipleship that has produced great ministries of human service and peacemaking. Others have seen their role as that of engaging in the total life of the community and seeking to transform it into something more in conformity to the Dominion of God.

All are attempts to be faithful. All fall prey to shortcomings either of becoming so separate that they have no effect as light and leaven in the dark world or being so involved that they are seduced and conformed. We live in the midst of the tragic, of the *chaos,* called to live and shine as lights in a dark world. This is the very essence of our *missionary incarnation,* namely being faithful to live and think and behave as people of New Creation, especially where the darkness and *chaos* is the greatest.

THE RESULT OF CONVERSION: HOLINESS

What God ultimately has in mind is a people who are in sync with himself. This harmony of being and purpose is what is embraced in the term *holiness.* Holiness is a life in which there is a growing experience of true beauty, true simplicity, true love and freedom. These are all dimensions of the creativity and newness of life. The whole of God's creation, the environment, and its stewardship become real. Mercy and justice move to the forefront of our concern for the human community.

Such holiness speaks to Chip and Generation X. Their sense of being *disposable* finds, in Jesus, true identity and roots into the eternal design of God. And where there has been a sense of *disconnectedness* and lack of true community, Jesus welcomes us into the very family of God. Human sexuality and bodily life find meaning under God's creative design and order. The purpose of human government is seen in God's gifts of peace and order and justice. Art flourishes in New Creation, as does music and mirth and dancing! The New Creation is freedom beyond imagining, and it is all found in that living relationship with God, through the Door who is Jesus Christ.

EIGHT

The Church: New Creation in Flesh and Blood

Somehow, we screwups still trying to find where the front door is ought to be able to see and experience a kind of community where all this Shalom happens in a kind of beautiful life together.

—Chip

It is of more than passing interest that when our Chip was living with a dull sense of dissatisfaction, and beginning to look for his heart's true home, that he wandered into a strange place with unknown people to see what *they* were doing there. It is also of more than passing importance that when Kate invited him to meet with some friends at her home that this became a place of attraction to Chip and the beginning of his journey into God's good news. Somehow the reality of a community of persons who have found *Shalom* in Jesus is very much a part of the reality of God's love for his own creation.

It is possible, conversely, for the local expression of the church itself to become the biggest stumbling block to this very quest for

God. Chip *could* get right up to the threshold of New Creation, only to be completely turned off by the contradictions between what Jesus taught and did and the church's behavior and attitude.

How much of the good news of God, of God's *Shalom,* of New Creation, is visible in the church? Such are not moot questions!

An outsider such as Chip has to get an honest answer to why the church even exists and how it is any part of what Jesus came to accomplish in rescuing us from *chaos.* The fact that the church *is,* and that it has always been somehow the community of the followers of Christ, is obvious enough. But what is its purpose in New Creation, in *salvation?* Is the church necessary to the gospel? These are the kinds of refreshing questions that Xers such as Chip have a proclivity for asking.

The answer in a nutshell to this second question: Yes! Without the church, the gospel is incomplete.

The New Creation, the Subversive Gospel, and the Church

As we seek to understand how to obey Jesus in the mission to reach the postmodern culture of Chip, Generation X, and Generation Y, the church moves very much to the forefront. Those who are deeply involved in this ministry have underscored the reality that for a generation that has known little of family or intimacy or of practical love, the very notion that *God really wants us in his family,* and has offered through Jesus Christ to actually *adopt* us into his caring family, catches their interest rather quickly.[1]

For a culture tired of hype, hustles, and words in general, it is going to be the demonstration of the gospel in the lives of followers of Jesus that will be most persuasive. When the gospel becomes visible in a community of grace that embraces with patience and love those who come with their cynicism, screwed-up lives, shame, and doubts; when that community has listening ears to hear questions and the heart's cry, then spiritually hungry men and women will also begin asking questions about, and listening for the voice of, the Good Shepherd.

Subversive Jesus, Radical Grace

In their world of disarray, of sullenness about institutions, government, the spoiled environment, the conflicts and violence, the hopelessness of so much of their existence, it is going to be the presence of communities of *Shalom*, of costly caring, of peacemaking, of beautiful ministries of justice, and of reverence for God's creation that will demand the attention of the most detached postmodern outsider.

THE CHURCH OVER PIZZA: A CONVERSATION _____

Over the weeks, Chip and his three new friends met together fairly regularly, sometimes for serious discussion, more often for meals or to play tennis. In the context of their growing friendship, honesty, and informality, they had been processing together all that we have been looking at in these previous chapters (and much more). One Saturday evening after a game of doubles, they were sitting together over pizza when Chip pushed them to the next level of his own search.

It is worth noting that Barbara, Kate, and Jong were enthusiastically walking with Chip on this search. They were all praying for him. They were aware that God was at work in Chip, and they were not trying to hurry the process. In fact, they had come to anticipate Chip's innocent candor and actually looked forward to where his search was taking him. Their authenticity enabled him to feel totally free with them.

"You know, guys, something doesn't fit," Chip said. "You make a pretty good case for Jesus. I like the idea of him coming to put together something radically new. If it's true—whatever *true* means—then a guy would assume that somewhere he could see it in operation and experience it. Right? I mean, if there's a great big bunch of you guys who have signed on with Jesus, and if somehow you were really into all the stuff we've been talking about, then you'd think that there would be excited *Exhibit A*'s all over the place. I would think it would be so overwhelming that it would really blow you away. If God is alive and present and awesome like you say he is, then I'd like to tune in and know what it's all about.

"I know I'm an outsider, and I may not know the password or

the secret handshake, but a while back when we were talking about how this whole thing came crashing down—you know, Adam and Eve and all that, the screwup and all the *chaos* that followed—one of the pieces that you told me about was the fracturing of the human community.[2] If I remember correctly, you described estrangement, broken relationships, indifference to persons, envy, and all kinds of destructive stuff. And because I lived my whole life with that fractured community and am a product of it, I'm more than mildly interested in the possibilities here. So if Jesus came to put it back together and to subvert that rebellion, how does he propose to recreate the human community so that it demonstrates this New Creation and allows me to experience it? Is it just talk, or is it real?

"Is that asking too much? Don't get mad at me here. I can even see that a guy's gotta be converted and all that. And I can begin to see what repentance and faith are all about. But it's gotta be more than just a bunch of individuals having some kind of a mystical and private inner experience. It has to be more tangible than a bunch of religious people running around spaced-out on Jesus and handing out some neat explanations with an invitation to join. Somehow, we screwups still trying to find the front door ought to be able to see and experience a kind of a community where all this *Shalom* happens in a kind of beautiful life together. Am I off-base?

"Let me push it a bit further, then I'll shut up. If a bunch of people, like you guys, really had seen how hopeless and dark their lives were when, as you explained to me, God got left out of the equation, and if you had renounced all of that chaotic and dehumanizing stuff (like we talked about a while back) and had come to follow Jesus, then shouldn't it *show* in ways so that guys like me could see, and smell, and experience it?[3] Can we talk about that? I mean, I know there is the church. But I don't make the connection between all we've been talking about and the church. It's big and there's lots of impressive institutional paraphernalia and stuff, but for me the church is sort of a contradiction, if not a stumbling block. Jesus and New Creation and all that good stuff, yes! Even the subversive and controversial bit we've talked about makes sense. Face it! I know I'm an outsider, though I'm getting closer, I think.

But I don't understand the church. What should I be looking for? Where would I see and experience it? What can I expect of a community of New Creation?"

Chip's three friends considered his final questions, and pondered them in silence for a few moments as they worked on their pizza.

"So, spell it out," Barbara responded. "What do you think it ought to look like? You've got to help us, Chip, because we're so accustomed to accepting the church as we've experienced it, as part of the normal Christian life, that I guess we're too blind to answer the question you've just handed us. What trips you up, and what would draw you further in?"

Chip sipped his drink and reflected for a minute. "Like, what would it look like, feel like, if a whole bunch of people put God squarely back into the heart of the human equation? What would it look like if not only did the individual person follow Jesus into hope and into *Shalom*, but the whole community lived and worked and related and cared because they were overwhelmed by God? What would it look like if God were real and awesome to them and if nothing was outside the arena of God's being present in them? And what would it look like if God's Word was really taken seriously?

"For instance, I'm an environmental engineer, and I live with the way we have really devastated the environment. And you say God is the Creator. All right. How, then, does God intend for you and the rest of his people to use and care for his creation? I mean, just for instance, if all the people who say they follow Jesus had a concern for the environment as God's creation, then there wouldn't be so much trashing of it, would there?"

"Now, there's a novel idea!" Kate chuckled.

That's how Chip pushed the others to take a fresh look at the community of New Creation. But it also raises the sobering reality that if the community of those who profess to follow Jesus doesn't demonstrate New Creation in some visible, alternative, and dramatic way, then outsiders have cause to doubt the whole of the message of Jesus!

THE CHURCH:
FORGETFULNESS AND FAITHFULNESS _____

The records of the church in the first generation after Jesus' sojourn with us reflect that it was precisely what Chip is requesting. It was a community that demonstrated Jesus, smelled like Jesus, looked like Jesus, and in which the experience of God was tangible and awesome. The good news of the Dominion of God did not just come with words, but with the Holy Spirit and with power.[4] The message was accompanied with signs and wonders. The awesomeness of the Lord was so much upon the whole community that no one dared join them unless he or she were really one of them. Even though the church was emerging into a very hostile world, it could not be ignored. When the messengers of this small but controversial new group came into one Grecian city, a public protest erupted because "these men who have turned the world upside down have come here also." Something unmistakable, transforming, and powerful was taking place in a community of ordinary men and women. No one could explain in mere human terms. But in the process of gaining new followers and a degree of acceptance, the church began to lose its alternative status.

The irony of a successful church is falling prey to its own success. The culture tends to coopt the church to its own ends ("If you can't beat 'em, join 'em!"). It is our human proclivity to weary of being different, of being aliens and strangers in this world. And when that happens, the church attempts to find ways to become comfortable, to be less confrontational, to smooth off the rough edges, and to settle down into coexistence with the world—and usually on the world's terms. It is because of this never-ending seduction that Jesus taught his followers to "watch and pray!"

Needless to say, whenever the church forgets its *raison d'être*, its Jesus-given reason to be, its calling to be about his God-given mission, or whenever it dilutes its message from its founding documents, then it reflects the *chaos* more than it does the New Creation! That this has happened and continues to happen is a reality we readily confess. Those outside the church have a predilection for seeking these contradictions within the church as some kind of a justification for their own rejection of its message. Conversely, the secular sources have great difficulty admitting the incredible manifestations of positive and redemptive ministries that have always flowed out of the church, even in some of its worst moments. It won't hurt our cause to catalog some of the negative and the positive demonstrations before we proceed.

The Bad News: Occasions When the Church Has Violated Its Own Calling

▶ *The official religion of the Roman Empire.* In the fourth century, the church was essentially coopted by Emperor Constantine and established as the primary religion of the Roman Empire. With this "Constantinianization" of the church, it essentially became the chaplain to the empire in return for the cessation of persecution. It is quite understandable, given three centuries of persecution, to see why the church was seduced by this honor. But it was also an accommodation that had tragic circumstances right down to the present moment.

> As the "established" church, it quickly succumbed to the *chaos,* to an idolatry of power. As it acquired wealth and property and created a *clergy-class* of ecclesiastical authorities, the church forgot its calling and mission.

▶ *The Crusades.* Later the church "blessed" the military crusades to punish the "infidels" who had taken possession of the Holy Land. In so doing, it demonized the Islamic peoples and made them the enemy rather than the objects of Christ's redemptive compassion. The tragedy of the crusades mars the church's perception of its missionary concern for the Islamic world to this day.

▶ *The Inquisitions.* In its zeal to maintain its power over thought, life, and ostensibly its purity of doctrine, the church exercised temporal power by ruthlessly suppressing anyone who voiced a difference or espoused a teaching that was not approved by "headquarters."[5] This resulted in the scandal of bloodshed, burnings at the stake, and injustices which contradict biblical teachings of how the church is to deal with those who forsake the message of New Creation.

▸ *Anti-Semitism.* While it was always acknowledged that the Jewish leadership of Israel was in a real way the initiator of the crucifixion of Jesus and that these same leaders made life miserable for the early church, over the centuries this developed into a full-blown antagonism and hatred toward the Jewish people as "Christ killers." This produced many forms of anti-Semitic persecutions, pogroms, and in the twentieth century, the Nazi holocaust. What a tragic contradiction of the church's calling to inherit the promise made to Abraham, that in his (Jesus') seed all the nations of the earth should be blessed! It contradicts Paul's own passion that his people Israel be saved. Anti-Semitism is a tragic violation of God's *Shalom.*

▸ *Indifference to injustice.* Whenever the church turns a blind eye to injustice, or a deaf ear to the cry of the crushed and marginalized of the world, it is a stark contradiction to the teachings of Jesus and the prophets. It means that the church has accommodated the *plausibility structures* of the society in which it lives. Whether this be indifference to slavery, to poverty and homelessness, economic discrimination in its many forms, or the rape of the environment, it is *all* a violation of God's heart, which seeks the blessing of his creation.

▸ *Ethnic cleansing and tribal hostilities.* In recent years we have witnessed such atrocities in Northern Ireland, Sudan, Rwanda, the Balkans, and elsewhere. People who wear the name of Jesus brutally, atavistically, bitterly persecute and kill those who are not of their tribe or religion. In many cases, it is followers of Christ who are killing each other!

The Good News:
Occasions When the Church Is Salt and Light

▸ *A people known for kingdom qualities.* For two millennia in untold thousands of local settings, in the most despicable and unlikely circumstances, followers of Jesus have loved and served and offered hospitality and blessed those around them. The world has never been the same since Jesus came, lived, died, and rose again. His followers, who have heard his calling and in whose lives he lives by his Spirit, have been the incarnation of the Sermon on the Mount; they have been people of mercy, of peacemaking, of generosity, of hope; so that *outsiders* have looked and tasted and acknowledged something very good. The Roman historian Pliny the Younger noted that the incredible reality of this suspect church was the depth of their love for each other, and their costly ministry to their neighbors.

▸ *Literacy and culture.* It was the church out of its devotion for Christ that became an instrument of education and culture, art and beauty. The recent book, *How the Irish Saved Civilization,* is a wonderful documentation of this truth. Patrick and the Irish monastics copied the great treasures of Roman and Greek civilization and so preserved the culture while the Goths destroyed the libraries of Rome and the ancient world. The Christian community was also the repository of treasures of both music and art.

▸ *Hospitality.* The medieval monasteries were places of hospitality and healing, as well as of gospel. They were the places of warmth and blessing and stability through a very tumultuous and unstable period. This has been true everywhere the church has gone. The New Creation mandate for taking in the homeless, feeding the hungry, clothing the naked, visiting the sick and prisoners has been a unique contribution to a very inhospitable world.

Ministries such as World Vision, Habitat for Humanity, Opportunity International, the Red

Cross, Voice of Calvary Ministries, the Mennonite Central Committee, some Roman Catholic orders, and many others have grown out of the vision of the followers of Christ seeing the needs of humankind and rising to bring solution, blessing, and gospel.

▶ *Justice.* Though it sometimes seems long in coming, it is the biblical focus on New Creation people as instruments of righteousness that has transformed so much of the larger society in which the church has taken root. Anglo-Saxon law was built upon the foundation of the Hebrew-Christian Scriptures. The anti-slavery movement in Great Britain grew out of a prayer meeting. Martin Luther King Jr. was a product of deep roots in the Christian faith, and it was to the church that he turned for support in bringing down the walls of segregation. Such stories have multiplied in countless ways across the globe.

▶ *Hope.* As the church has been light and leaven in the darkness of the world, it has also been a community that has quietly brought meaning in the midst of meaninglessness, truth in the confusing voices of the *chaos*, and hope when there appeared no hope.

It is important to register such fruits because, as I have stated, in the task of reaching those still outside, the foibles of the church are exaggerated by the darkness, while the incomparable blessings and contributions frequently go unnoticed.

THE MYSTERY OF THE CHURCH

If the church is enigmatic to outsiders such as Chip, it is also a grand mystery. To look at its history as a missionary community is more than fascinating. To see Jesus Christ actually building his church as he promised he would creates awe. The mystery is that God works in ways that are often strange and "left-handed."

The church has always been a mystery, a mixture of faithfulness and unfaithfulness, of both contradictions and unbelievable moments of splendor. Someone cryptically observed that the surest evidence of the divine character of the church is that it has survived its human leadership. And that's just the point. What assures us that this thing called the church, with all of its foibles and accomplishments, is not only going to be there but will be the determinative force in history, is that it is Jesus himself who is building it. It's *his!* The recreation of true community is part and parcel of his good news. He is the one who calls it into being; and he is the one who is present by the Spirit to refine and empower, and bring it to its consummation. Jesus told his infant church unequivocally: "Without me you can do nothing." And the evidence of that continues to erupt in unexpected ways and unexpected places.

For the past two millennia the followers of Jesus have professed to believe that the church, wherever it exists, is God's, formed by the teachings of Jesus passed along by the apostles. In one of the ancient creeds, that truth is expressed as: "I believe in the one, holy, catholic and apostolic church."[6] In every generation from the beginning people have asked the very question that Chip is asking.

It is also true that because the church consists of normal and fallible human beings, from time to time and in various places it forgets who it is and why it exists. When this happens, it goes from being a viable, healthy community of the Dominion of God to a sick, if not dead, one! But because it is Jesus who is building the church, and though a particular community or missionary movement may falter, he raises up other faithful communities to carry on the mission.

It is all the more fascinating that when the church's light grows very dim, when its witness to Christ is difficult to discern, when its professing members mirror the darkness around them, there still echo remnants of days of faithfulness. In the moribund church community there are the magnificent liturgies and traditions with all their riches of adoration and affirmation. In great cathedrals and many older church buildings are magnificent stained glass windows containing stories of the gospel, biblical personalities, missionary heroes, and great church leaders. In the church's stories and hymns, profound faith and faithfulness are evident, even if such are not present reality. The mystery of the church!

THE CHURCH: WHAT SHOULD IT LOOK LIKE, SMELL LIKE, BEHAVE LIKE? _____

If on one hand we can accept Chip's challenge that the church ought to "look and smell and behave like" New Creation, and on the other hand we stand back and look at our calling and purpose, then we might gain helpful clues to improve the church's effectiveness in the postmodern culture.

Such descriptions of smelling and looking may obviously sound strange to many, but they are not strange to the biblical documents. "But thanks be to God, . . . in Christ and through us spreads everywhere the fragrance of the knowledge of him. For we are to God the aroma of Christ among those who are being saved and those who are perishing."[7] According to Paul, the church is called to be God's glory just as Jesus is![8] The church is the body of Christ, the physical presence of the reality of Christ to each generation by its word and behavior. The followers of Christ, who are the church, are to be imitators of Christ as dear children. The world is not to be bereft of that presence which exudes the aroma of Christ and reflects his light in the midst of this age of death.

What is more, in the early church and in times of faithfulness in the intervening centuries, there has been that wholesome and awesome reality about the church which is called "the fear of God." There is a reverence, a sense of God's presence and power, of transcendence. And that experience of transcendence is very much a part of the longings of the emerging generation.

There are three dimensions or descriptions of the church that we need to explore: (1) the church as the Community of the Messiah, of the Dominion of God in Christ; (2) the church as an Alternative Community, as Redeemed Society; and (3) the church as a Mission Community, as God's Agent of Blessing the Nations.

Subversive Jesus, Radical Grace

The Community of the Messiah

Paul told the Corinthian believers that they were "the aroma of Christ unto God." For those of us who are the present-day church, this means we must be consumed with the adoration of Jesus, the Lamb of God, so much so that it permeates our lives and behavior. We must be informed and formed by who Jesus is, what he has done in rescuing us for God, how he loves and thinks and how his heart beats when he looks upon *all* of his Father's world. The church must continually embrace the worship of Christ that the church has embraced from its beginning. We must never mute "the song of Moses the servant of God and the song of the Lamb."[9]

It is when the church becomes preoccupied with its institutional form or agendas other than those given by Jesus that it begins to be inhabited by the darkness. Tragically, it is this very preoccupation that has equivocated the church's calling time and again. When the sweet aroma of Christ is diluted with vague religiosity, generic spirituality, or noble agendas not motivated out of love and adoration for him, then though the aroma may be a refreshing change from the smell of death around it, it still misses the point and truncates its calling to be the very body of Christ here in the human community.

As anointed Son of the living God, Jesus promised that he himself would build his church. The infant church acknowledged that:

> *He is the image of the invisible God, the firstborn over all creation. For by him all things were created: things in heaven and on earth, visible and invisible, whether thrones or powers or rulers or authorities; all things were created by him and for him. He is before all things, and in him all things hold together. And he is the head of the body, the church; he is the beginning and the firstborn from among the dead, so that in everything he might have the supremacy. For God was pleased to have all his fullness dwell in him, and through him to reconcile to himself all things, whether things on earth or things in heaven, by making peace through his blood, shed on the cross.[10]*

Any *outsider,* any wanderer looking for his or her heart's true home, who comes into proximity of the community of New Creation must never miss the point that everything about this New Creation is done out of its joyous trust in Jesus. The church that desires to *smell like Jesus* must always be beholding and reflecting the Lord's glory and so be continually transformed into his glory. This glory of the Lord is made known in the face of Christ.[11]

In the Christian mystery of the Triune God, the Father is glorified in the Son, the Son glorifies the Father, the Spirit witnesses to the Son. And in the mystery of the church, the church abides in Christ and Christ abides in the church by his Word and Spirit. Christ is then glorified in and by his church and the church is motivated by the glory of God in Christ. It is a community of worship. Jesus, who loves and adores the Father, dwells in his people so that he through them (us) worships and glorifies the Father. The church finds its ultimate reason for being in worship.

According to John 17, Jesus prayed that his newborn church will experience his *joy;* that they will know *truth* as it is made known in and by him; that they will move into the world in the same *mission* of God, which sent him into the world; that they will experience a true *unity,* a restored oneness and intimacy, reflecting the intimacy within the Trinity; that they will be the agents of God's *glory* even as Jesus is; and that they will be inundated with his own divine *love.* All of this is experienced *in Christ,* and gives us some understanding of what the sweet aroma of Christ smells like. The very notion of being *born again* carries with it the implication that somehow, by the working of God, the family likeness of God is created in ordinary human beings. God's family bears the family characteristics.

The process of being transformed from children of darkness into children of Light, however, is not some mindless, otherworldly, mystical experience. Worshiping Jesus always involves *knowledge.* We are recreated into the image of God in *knowledge.* This means that in the church, the community of New Creation, teaching the biblical narrative, especially the words of Jesus and his apostles, is the agent by which this New Creation emerges. The church's traditional formula says that true and saving faith involves *knowledge* of Jesus, *assent* to who he is and what he taught and did on the cross, and *faith-trust* that embraces him. When this takes place, the followers of Christ have assurance that they have "the mind of Christ" or "the mind of the Spirit."[12] Such confidence is not arrogant, but thinking in harmony with the one who called the church into being.

This New Creation in Jesus is also very visible. As Jesus lives in his followers, his heart of compassion beats within them. It is not at all surprising that because Jesus' inaugural sermon reflected the heart of God toward the poor and crushed of the human community, the first special gift or office created in the early church was that of the *deacon,* specifically to care for those who were economically helpless and ethnically discriminated against. This *diaconal* ministry is Christ, by his own Spirit, living out the compassion of God in his community of *Shalom.*

When an outsider such as Chip looks at the phenomenon known as "the church," he or she may be quite confused. The church often makes its institutional life a thing-in-itself and fails to reflect the character of God in its works. But the *knowledge* of God communicated in the biblical documents tunes us in to a whole new way of life. So we segue now into the alternative character of the community of Jesus.

An Alternative Community, A New Humanity

The command to *repent,* which stands at the threshold of true faith, is the calling to morally (or volitionally) disengage oneself from the tyranny of that dominion which ignores the glory and purpose of God *(chaos),* and to enter into a new identity as a citizen of the Dominion of God's dear Son. Paul calls this our death to sin, and our resurrection to new life in Christ. It is a decision to renounce our slavery to the life that leaves God out of the human equation and a decision to become slaves of what is right, of justice.

To accept Christ's *totalitarian* claim on our lives makes the church a radically different community. The public sign of *baptism,* by which we enter this community, symbolizes being buried with Christ to sin and rising with him to a whole new kind of life marked by the Cross. It is a radical decision to be identified with [the *subversive*] Christ in the service of righteousness.[13]

Whenever the followers of Jesus begin to name the idols of this *chaos,* of this world of distorted values and false gods, we are in essence challenging the power of the deceiver, the prince of this world. These idols are not benign. There are nationalistic and tribal idols, military idols, economic idols, idols of greed, idols of pleasure, idols of comfort, idols of "rights," philosophical and intellectual idols, even idols of college or company or church organization![14] Sad to say, such challenges are seldom made. The idols are too often embraced and moved into a place of worship right alongside God. The result: The church becomes conformed to the world, and nobody knows the church even exists! The smell of death prevails, and God weeps. Repentance is thereby contradicted and baptismal vows denied.

The practical and realistic implications of such repentance are impossible to hide. Jesus' own words are that all who love him will keep his commandments. His commission to his infant church is to teach men and women to obey all that he had commanded. This means that the agenda of the Dominion of God, of New Creation, with all of its individual, social, communal, political, economic, environmental, and holistic dimensions, becomes the lifestyle of the church. Such a calling to repentance is a calling to be the very embodiment of the prophetic teachings of Jesus, as he stood in the direct line with the Old Testament prophets. It means becoming involved with God in God's own compassion for those who are victims of the system, homeless, crushed economically and politically, deprived of life's necessities. Such a church has the aroma of Christ. It looks and feels like that which Jesus was and taught.

Is such an aroma what our Chip is wondering about? Unquestionably. Is it evangelism? Absolutely. When men and women begin to see New Creation in action and to ask questions about why this is so, then God is at work drawing them to himself. When those outside begin to ask a reason for the hope that is in the church, the church's word about Jesus is coming in power.

In a society that has the proclivity to ignore any responsibility to the lostness and need of others, the church is, above all, that alternative which is the embodiment of the love of God for all persons.

Subversive Jesus, Radical Grace

The darkness always resists the Light. The last book in the Bible, the Revelation, is a pastoral guide to the church about the warfare that wages between the forces of the Beast (with all of the destructive energy given to him) and the Lamb. It graphically portrays the anti-Christ religions and anti-Christ political powers that battle the faithful practitioners of the Christ's teachings. In this period in which we live, between the ages, we must realize that while Jesus has triumphed over principalities and powers on his cross, the final destruction of the Wicked One awaits. Meanwhile, suffering is part of the calling to be an alternative people. We obey in an alien context, and, more often than not, we don't win. But we are promised that even when we fail, we are more than conquerors through Christ. To suffer for what is good enables us to share in the sufferings of Christ.

At the same time, Jesus taught us to pray: "Lead us not into testing, and deliver us from the evil one." Peter told the infant church that they should not be surprised at the fiery trials which awaited them, and that if and when they were so insulted because of Christ, then they could know that the Spirit of glory and of God was upon them.[15] This also is part of the aroma of Christ in his New Creation, part of the visible and experience-able community of *Shalom*. Again, this leads us to that other reality of the church, that it is a mission community.

Hope and the Mission of God

It is precisely because the sweet aroma of *faith* lingers about the church, and precisely because the sweet aroma of Christ's extravagant *love* is daily exhibited in the church, that it can also have the sweet aroma of *hope* about it. Jesus Christ has been raised from the dead, and because of that, nothing is "locked-in"; all things are now possible. Hope is that essential sense of being called by Christ to participate in what God is doing in the world. It is the energizing confidence that the church is the agent of God's power and of God's future and redemptive design for his creation. But hope that is seen is not hope. The church lives as the sweet aroma of Christ in a horribly ambiguous and often malignant human society.

When Jesus told his followers: "As the Father has sent me, even so do I send you," he was creating a *mission community*, not a religious institution. He was sending them to be light in the darkness, to seek out places where the glory of his Father was defiled, there to demonstrate light and truth and love and hope. As Christ became flesh and blood in the midst of the needs of humankind, so the church locates its life and relocates its life precisely to be the presence of God's light and love in those corrupted places. Each new generation and generational culture becomes the arena of this New Creation.

God came to us when we were enemies, and through his reconciling grace in Jesus Christ took away the offense and restored us to himself as sons and daughters. The church's mission is to make that same reconciliation known among those who live with a sense of guilt and separation; it encompasses the ministry of breaking down the walls of hostility between individuals, communities, tribes, nations, and traditions, wherever destructive anger and brokenness exist.

Such a mission sometimes entails costly solutions. So it is that Jesus teaches his New Creation people to make their lives and fortunes and skills available to those in need. So it is that an agency such as Habitat for Humanity redistributes wealth and skills in providing decent homes for people without them. So it is that communities of Christians provide agencies for job training or for making low-interest loans to small entrepreneurs, or engage in ministries to families in crisis or hospitality to refugees. It is because of this mission that medical groups make their skills available to those folk who otherwise would be helpless in the face of illness and disease. It is when the church sees the crime and corruption of neighborhoods and cities that Christian urban pioneers, laying aside their security and profit, move again into those places where their services are so desperately needed.

The very fact that God's people know why this world exists and where it is going gives them the aroma of hope when all around appears hopeless. As Christ's followers care for each other, they produce a wholesome community of intimacy (κοινονια). And it is by such love that Jesus tells them that *outsiders* will know that they are his disciples. The relationships within the community of New Creation are intended to demonstrate restored humanity to the world. These relationships are to be caring, redemptive, reconciling, purposeful, generous, and celebrative.

In what is often a dismal history of the church's unfaithfulness, there stand forth in beautiful contrast those numerous and encouraging episodes in which committed Christian people once again hear the call and give themselves to be communities of faith, hope, and love. They know that God has spoken in Jesus Christ. They know that to follow him is to be a recreated people. They know that the Lamb of God is worthy of their lives of obedience. They move into the darkness and among *outsiders* with hope, trusting that those *outside* will see and smell and know that God somehow is at work.

When words become empty, as they are in our cynical culture, it is the life of the community of New Creation that communicates God's design to those seeking their heart's true home. It is Christ living by his own Spirit in his people. It is the church.

The Breath of God

*Even if I wanted to believe the stuff you say Jesus
makes possible, you know, like being a part of the
enticing idea of New Creation, I just don't have it in
me. I'm back to my initial "yeah, right" response.*

—Chip

"Uh, like, wait just a minute. Something here doesn't fit. I
mean, the world is full of Utopian idealists, lots of do-
gooders running around trying to make it all perfect. And when any
presidential candidate runs on a platform of peace and justice and
love, he doesn't even make it past single digits in the polls. This is
not to mention all of the altruists with burnout. So all of the stuff
we've been talking about New Creation and *Shalom* really has a
nice sound, except that it is so alien to my whole delightfully self-
indulgent, comfortable, oversexed, and totally meaningless way of
life! Even if I wanted to believe the stuff you say Jesus makes possible, you know, like being a part of the enticing idea of New Creation, I just don't have it in me. I'm back to my initial 'yeah, right'
response. Sitting here, I'm torn. I see something in you guys, and
hear something that triggers deep longings. But then I say: 'It'll
never work.' Any response?"

Such was Chip's next salvo at his friends.

At this, Barbara burst into laughter and clapped her hands.

"Chip, I love you. I've been waiting for you to raise this question. You're so beautifully honest. I just love it." She went on to explain to him that his refreshingly honest protest had opened the door to another often neglected, yet incredibly wonderful dimension of God's good news to those captive to the *chaos*. This was a necessary step in Chip's pilgrimage.

We must remind ourselves again that Chip is a part of a spiritually hungry generation, obsessed with a vague quest for an experience of the transcendent, some liminal *spirituality* to assuage their emptiness. Thus their focus on meditation and New Age and Eastern religions, all in an effort to fulfill that subjective and ill-defined "something" that haunts their silences.

THE MYSTERY OF THE AWESOME SPIRIT OF GOD ____

Chip's friends were very affirming of his protest. Then they walked with him into God's own affirmation of his point. Jesus had a very specific role to play in becoming the Door into God's New Creation and of making that entrance possible by his own life and death on the cross. But he also knew that the radical transformation necessary both as New Creation persons and New Creation communities was not at all possible with merely human resources. The *chaos* was too determinative. So in the final days of his earthly sojourn with his disciples, Jesus opened the door to the next dimension of his *salvation* by introducing the promise of his own Spirit, the Spirit of Life, the Spirit of Truth, the Spirit of the Father and of the Son. In what could only have been considered an enigmatic comment by his disciples, Jesus told them he would not leave them "desolate," but that it was actually essential that he leave them (after his resurrection) and go to the Father so that the Spirit could come.[1] They weren't going to be left without his own dynamic and transforming presence, but this time it would be in the role of the Spirit of God.

What makes this all the more fascinating (Barbara, Kate, and Jong rehearsed this history with Chip) is that centuries earlier, the prophets of Israel had introduced the reality of the Spirit. As the prophets opened up the promise of the coming age of God's anointed servant, an awesome part of that promise was that God would no longer make his will known on written tablets, but would write it into the hearts of his new people by his own Spirit. He promised a "new spirit" and the power of a whole new kind of life to them when the New Covenant (the Dominion of God) unfolded at the coming of God's anointed messenger.[2] When Jesus talked to inquirers such as Nicodemus about being "born again," he was speaking of the necessity of a transforming dynamic by which a person would be indwelt by God's Spirit, and would see with God's eyes and hear with God's ears.[3] This is not even remotely possible by merely human religious resources.

It gets more awesome at this point. Chip has unwittingly opened the door for us to enter the *mystery* of the Triune God, who is Father, Son, and Holy Spirit. And that door also reveals to us the missionary intent of God from start to finish, but from a bit different perspective. That God so loved the world that he gave his Son is well known to the church. How it was necessary for the Holy God to deal with the alienation and condemnation that resulted from human sin and rebellion. But even that has roots all the way back into God's Word of promise to Abraham two millennia before Jesus: "In your seed shall all of the nations of the earth be blessed." God had, after all, commissioned ancient Israel to be a missionary people, to be a "nation of priests" so that the whole world should know of the one true God.[4] They forgot. God gave Israel rules and a covenant about how to be a holy people and thus reflect his glory and purpose among the nations. They failed.

The sending of the Son to be sin-bearer, the inaugurator of God's dominion and his new and everlasting covenant, was then the necessary centerpiece of God's message of his love for the whole world. Jesus was visible and vocal. He was, and is, God-man. He lived and taught and demonstrated the glory of God. He suffered the hostility of humankind on one hand, and the wrath of God against human sin on the other. He became the means of our reconciliation with God, the one who purchased our forgiveness. In him we are made clean and adopted into the Father's family. So far, so good.

But God did not then stand back and say: "There, that's done.

Let's see what these followers of Jesus do with that." Not at all. God's purpose is a *mission* purpose. It is his sovereign design that this good news of New Creation shall be known among the nations, that he be glorified in every people group. He is not only active, but aggressive in seeing to it that this mission is accomplished. We have been using the term *subversive* to describe the intent of God to bring about something radically new and redemptive. So all that we are observing, and will observe, about the Spirit of God has both God's *mission* and God's *subversive* intent.

When we consider the fact that pagan cultures and mythologies are replete with beliefs in spirits and sprites and fairies — mysterious noncorporeal beings not confined to time and space — the notion of *spirit* is not all that strange to our postmodern minds. And pagan cultures are at least receptive to the mysteries of life, nature, and the unseen, more so than much of the Christian culture. But when Jesus gives his followers his Spirit, it is not for some self-absorbed spirituality or for some otherworldly escape. Rather it is part and parcel of his *subversive* agenda. The Spirit of God is the Creator Spirit.

What Chip's friends shared with him (and needs to be remembered by the followers of Jesus) is that God, who is the Creator of all, is not in any way confined to time and space, or to the visible and tangible. God is not confined to a body. So when Jesus began to hint to his followers that he would not be with them *physically* much longer (not confined to one body), it should not be unbelievable that he could be present with them in some other way. The unseen Spirit would usher in a reality beyond anything they had ever thought or imagined. This giving of the Spirit to his followers flowed out of God's purpose to bring about *Shalom* and to transform (or recreate) both persons and communities. He never intended to be an absentee object of faith!

What Chip cannot see and does not begin to realize is the awesome power at work to make God's New Creation happen, to make it work, namely the sovereign Spirit of the Father and the Son turned loose in the world. Or as one New Testament writer states it: "him who is able to do immeasurably more than all we ask or imagine,

Subversive Jesus, Radical Grace

according to *his power that is at work within us*"[5] This is to say that the power of God is dynamically present and at work within the community called the church, in order to demonstrate to the world the kingdom of God, and the will of God, just as did God's Son, Jesus Christ. And this power, this glory, is the Spirit of the sovereign Lord. The Spirit is the fulfillment of Jesus' promise that even as all authority had been given him, so he would be with his followers in their obedience to his mission until the end of the age.

The Spirit of God is even more difficult for us to comprehend than the Son of God precisely because the Spirit is noncorporeal, nonphysical, invisible. At the same time, we have to understand the role of the Spirit in continuity with what God was and is doing in Christ. If Jesus would say to his followers, "Even as the Father has sent me, even so do I send you," then we have to look at the promise of the Spirit as having the dynamic role in making that happen.[6] And the purpose of God's Dominion through Christ is to *subvert the subversion,* in other words, to redeem creation from the distortion and defilement caused by the rebellion, the *chaos.* John explained that Jesus came to destroy the works of the Devil. Same thing.

It's like Jesus saying: "Listen guys, I've got to go away. But I'm not going to leave you here swinging in the wind. I'm sending you to do the humanly impossible work of making disciples of every people group in this dark world, and you can never do this with merely human resources. But don't sweat it. I am going to come to you (as a matter of fact, both my Father and I are going to come to you) by my Spirit, who will be with you in power and with all of my authority. The Spirit will enable you to be and do what is humanly unimaginable, precisely so that the glory of God that is demonstrated in me will be demonstrated in you as the church (which I will be building). The *kingdom works* which I have done, you will do also, and even more than I have done. The Spirit will be at work in you to provide all that you need. He will bring glory to me by bringing everything I have said to your minds. He will keep you focused on me and will testify of me. Everything that belongs to my sovereign Father is mine. And the Spirit will take from my riches and make it all known to you. Got it?"

The Spirit and the New Humanity in Christ ____

Once Jesus is embraced by faith, then the new life by the Spirit of Jesus begins to work inwardly to form or create a whole new race, a new humanity.[7] Because Jesus is the door into the Father's house, into the Dominion of God, one of the first things that one encounters is the overwhelming and compelling reality of it all. This ultimate reality is not seen by merely human eyes. The *eyes* given by the Spirit do, in fact, begin to see and understand that this Dominion is the only certain and eternal Dominion, and this puts all other lords and loyalties, all other pretenders to ultimacy, in their true perspective. The glory of God in all of God's creation, the doing of God's will above all others, these become sealed in the believer's conscience and mind.

What results is a people who defy human rationale—joyful obedience when there appears no human cause for joy; hope when there is no apparent reason to hope; peace not as the world gives; self-denying love because we have been so loved; gentleness in the midst of arrogance; faithfulness in the midst of fickleness; and self-control in the midst of self-indulgence. What starts to grow are the strength and gentleness of Christ in ordinary men and women; *Sermon on the Mount living,* which flies in the face of all of the consumer culture that permeates our society; generosity that is free to give away; and flexibility that is free to relocate in order to be and do that which will glorify Christ and minister his blessings in areas of need. All because of the new birth by the Spirit!

What we're talking about here, by the way, is also known as *holiness,* being *in sync* with the character of God. And it is the working of the *Holy* Spirit to accomplish such transformation.

Transformed men and women know they are sent by Jesus for the very same purpose that Jesus was sent by the Father. They display a boldness that has no fear of death or loss. They identify with the Cross of Christ and the Word of Christ which make them overcomers no matter what. They are a whole new and alternative humanity living right in the midst of the old. To enter God's Dominion is to enter a missionary calling and to be accompanied by the sovereign Spirit who is not confined to human categories, who is not confined to the church, *who is not confined!* The Spirit energizes not only the vision and the motivation, but also the moral and volitional obedience over all human reason.

So the questions and incredulity which Chip verbalizes are *gifts* to anyone looking with compassion at those who are still outside of God's family and at the ministry of communicating the good news of Jesus and the Dominion of God to them. You know what? Chip is absolutely right. It would all seem quite impossible except for the fact that Jesus not only delivers us from our captivity to the *chaos* by his work on the Cross, but once he opens that prison-cell door and once we walk into his embrace, he also gives us his own life, his *power of the resurrection* in order to conform us to his own image. This is another of the incredible gifts of God: his own Spirit to work in us the process of conforming us to, and making us participants in, his New Creation.

But it certainly does *look* unlikely. And were we left to our merely human resources, it would be ridiculous to even begin. We keep falling into that trap. We keep thinking of doing it all with our own frail human resources. What Jesus knew and what he taught is that he knows far more profoundly and realistically than we can ever imagine how complex and enslaving and destructive is the *chaos* into which we were born. He knows how that *chaos* continually seeks to seduce us and to conform us again to itself. Jesus understands this present age and its blindness to real *reality.* He knows how deaf its inhabitants are to true *truth*, and to any propaganda except its own. He knows all of this so that the whole *subversion,* which he turned loose by his cross, is totally and insanely impossible . . . unless he somehow accompanies it with his own authority and presence in actual experience. This is the working of the Spirit of Christ in us.

This is not only *high mystery,* not only *holy ground,* but it blows one's mind!

The very notion that Jesus Christ, the sovereign Lord, is very much alive and present and active everywhere in the world means that he is inescapable. It means that he is everywhere present as both the Giver of Life and as the Consuming Fire. Here is the Son of

God risen from the dead, the Anointed of God by whom and for whom all things are created, telling his followers that they will actually do greater works than he has done. Somehow, God is going to be personally and corporately present with them after Jesus departs physically. Mysterious? Yes! Sobering? You'd better believe it!

THE NEW CREATION, THE CHURCH, AND THE SPIRIT

As it is crucial for us to remember that Jesus came to inaugurate this New Creation, so it is also crucial to remember that the reality of the Spirit, and the community which the Spirit creates, is not in any way disconnected from that missionary purpose of Jesus. The inauguration of the Dominion of God is by the person and work of Jesus, who flings open the door into God's embrace. But the dynamic presence of that self-same Dominion is by the working of the Spirit of the Father and the Son. The Spirit is sent, out of the infinite love and grace of God, for the very purpose that Chip stumbles over; namely, to *make it happen.* The Spirit is given for the creation of that reality which is in harmony with the mind and will of God. The working of Jesus, and of the Spirit of Jesus, is not for some private spiritual experience (though he does work privately and individually) apart from New Creation. Rather, the working of the Spirit is to create agents of that New Creation, and to create the Community of New Creation, and to energize these for ministry as colaborers with him.

When Jesus teaches his followers, "Seek first the Dominion of God and his justice-righteousness, and all of these things shall be added unto you," he is not giving them a formula for personal security and provision.[8] Rather, Jesus is telling his followers that as they live out the *subversive* missionary agenda of the Sermon on the Mount, and live out the costly mandates of this New Creation before the world, that God will be with them to provide necessities. Somehow, all of Jesus' teachings about the Spirit are linked with love for him and with obedience to him in his mission. So the Spirit of God and the mission of God are integrally connected.

The church is the community of that mission, and of that Spirit and of that New Creation.

The church has frequently gotten tangled up in, or lost in, fruitless debates about how men and women enter into God's great salvation and become new creatures in Christ. How does the change take place? Who is, and who isn't, part of God's plan? What such debates frequently overlook is the sovereign power of God in the mission of God. It overlooks his infinite love which *wills* all men everywhere to repent and obtain his forgiveness.[9] Such debates also overlook the omnipresent workings of God's Spirit. It was the Spirit of God who brooded upon the waters in the creation of the world. It is the Spirit of God who works through history to incline humankind's hearts to God's purposes, or to harden their hearts for the same purpose. It is the Spirit of God who creates the church!

To use another metaphor, imagine a *divine energy field* (or a *divine force field*) all around Jesus. To come into proximity of Jesus—whether physically, or by the preaching of Christ, or the community of faith living by the Spirit—is to come into proximity with that energy field. John said of Jesus, "He came to his own creation and that his own creation did not receive him, . . . yet to all who received him, who believed in his name, he gave the right to become the children of God."[10] What does that mean? It means that Jesus is the *Way* to God, and that to embrace Jesus (through repentance and faith) is to come into that energy field of God by which sinful men and women become subjects of the Spirit's recreating power. And that recreating power begins to conform them to the image of the Son of God. They begin to see like Jesus. They begin to hear like Jesus. They begin to respond to God the Father in adoration as Jesus did. They begin to have that zeal to obey the Father's will and to do the mandates of the Dominion of God just as Jesus did.

This becomes more awesome when we stop to consider just how impervious the human heart can be to the voice of God and the reality of God. In what is a very unflattering description, Paul told the followers of Jesus in Asia Minor that they were "dead in [their] transgressions and sins," that they were captives to the ways of the world, and to the spiritual powers of darkness, totally at the mercy of their chaotic appetites. But, he went on to say that in Christ they had been given sight, brought to life from the dead, not by any merit of their own, but by the sovereign grace of God. And as those made alive to God, they were now to be the agents and demonstrations of his goodness and mission in the world, people of New Creation.[11]

New life in Christ is made possible by the working of the Spirit of Christ in ordinary human beings. It is a gift of God, not just a "spiritual trip." It is being brought into *sync* with God's wonderful missionary purpose. It is holistic. It causes weak human vessels to be filled with the transcendent power and glory of God.[12] So as Chip circles around the Word of Christ being given to him by his friends, he is in proximity to the Spirit's energy field, and there is a centripetal force created by the Spirit that draws him inward. The Spirit accompanies the obedient church as it seeks to express Christ's compassion for those outside.

This is what makes the preaching of Christ so crazy, or foolish, in the eyes of the world. What it does is to bring unsuspecting hearers into the energy field of the Spirit! (If you were to take the reality of the Spirit out of the missionary accounts of the New Testament, it would all deflate into a merely human enterprise . . . and utterly fail!) Paul described the hearers as those blinded by the god of this age, lest they hear and see. But, he added, the God who called upon the light to shine in the primordial darkness at creation is the same God who by his Spirit causes the light of Christ to shine in hearts. And what is the role of the human witness? The Spirit enables this dependent and weak witness to communicate the facts of Christ (the Word of Christ) faithfully. Nothing else. God is at work by his Spirit to bring life from the dead.[13]

It is the visible human community *restored* to its true purpose as a dimension of the gospel which Chip is asking about. This is exactly why the life of the church is so critical to the task of reaching those outside. The Spirit of God *goes before* the Word, making ears and hearts ready. He *goes with* the communication of the Word, making it alive and compelling against all human reason. The Spirit *works through* the Word to create New Creation people who are captive to the love of God and are being recreated into his likeness in knowledge, right living, and holiness. The Spirit *fills* his people with joy, and *gives* them a self-denying love for each other. He also gives them compassionate eyes for those who are outside, those who are victims of injustice, those who are marginalized and in need of food and clothing and shelter. He creates zeal for those who are lost and seeking their heart's true home, that they know of God's love in Christ.

This New Creation community is the community of true *Shalom*. By the Spirit men and women are equipped to live obediently, interdependently, responsibly under the Word of Christ and by the enabling of the Spirit. It is the kind of true intimacy and caring and purposeful community that we are created for. It is the community called the church for which Christ gave his life and for which he sends his Spirit. The aroma of the church by the Spirit is the aroma of Christ.

The point to be made here is that the Spirit accompanies the proclamation of the *radical* message of the Dominion of God and creates an alternative people empowered to live out its *subversive* agenda within the human community. There is created that living presence of the redefined *power* which works in quiet, servantlike, self-denying obedience to the design of God's New Creation. The Spirit creates a people who are effective because they are marked by the Cross, and even when they lose or are killed, they are more than conquerors. This *quiet revolution*[14] is an evangelistic witness to those outside, but it is also the creation of a powerful and transformational community in the Spirit that demonstrates God's love and God's will to the whole.

Chip has come into proximity to this *divine energy field* and has experienced something of its power in the persons of his new friends. And they are at the same time those agents of the Risen Lord and of his Spirit inviting Chip to enter through the Door who is Christ and to realize what the church has experienced for these two millennia, namely that the Dominion of God is not just talk, but rather transforming power of the Spirit of God![15]

Tears and Laughter Between the Ages

Is there a downside to all of this? If I were to take the plunge and join you in following Jesus, are there negatives I ought to know upfront?

—Chip

C hip was too savvy to jump without looking. The answer to his question voiced above is very clear: *Yes!* With Chip, with the work of evangelism, it is unconscionable to suggest that to follow Christ is possible without the Cross, without any further suffering. There is pain associated with the gospel. One of the promises of Jesus that gets far too little currency is:

> *If you belonged to the world, it would love you as its own. As it is, you do not belong to the world, but I have chosen you out of the world. That is why the world hates you. . . . If they persecuted me, they will persecute you also. . . . They will treat you this way because of my name.*[1]

The evangelistic discipline is quite dishonest and ill-informed if it suggests that the new life in Christ is without dissonances, or conflicts, or heartaches, or ambiguities, or doubts, or unimaginable confrontations with the *chaos* and the expressions of the darkness, all of which can reduce us to human despair.[2]

But having said that, let me hasten to say that at the very same time we are in despair at a human level, at a much deeper level, *by the Spirit,* we also tap into a profound resonance with the very embrace of the living God. In the midst of our tears we come to know the "peace that passes human understanding." We experience the joy of the Lord.

Still, this does not mean that the tears are less real, nor the pain less severe. What it *does* mean is that we are sharing in the very same pain and tears and suffering, and for the same reasons, that our Lord Jesus Christ wept and agonized. We become sharers in the sufferings of Christ.[3] This is all very much a part of the church's calling to the mission of God. And if those sufferings are nowhere present in our experience, it should caution us to look carefully at our faithfulness.[4] The teachings of Peter are a good place for us to begin to look at this dimension of the evangelistic task. Peter reminds us that the community of New Creation is always a community of aliens and strangers for the very reason that it is a holy nation, and thus out of sync with the world.

The question about pain and persecutions can only be a stumbling block if we have a truncated understanding of the *evangel!* You may ask why in the world anyone would oppose the message of forgiveness of sins, the love of God, or of doing good? The answer is very simple. Such pieces of the gospel are not the whole gospel. To declare only these pieces is not being faithful to the New Testament message of Jesus.

We need to be reminded that unless we have preached: (1) the *data* of the gospel, (2) the *demands* of the gospel, and (3) the *promises* of the gospel, we have not preached the gospel! The world can easily ridicule the Christian faith as "pie in the sky by and by" or as being "so heavenly minded that it is of no earthly use." The *plausibility structures,* or the *dominant social orders,* of this world can easily accommodate the Christian community and its faith as long as these are economically, or politically, or socially useful to their causes. But when the holistic gospel of the Dominion-Kingdom of God is

Subversive Jesus, Radical Grace

taught and practiced, then a clash of dominions occurs, and these worldly structures become first restive, then hostile. As long as New Creation is no threat to these powers, they see it as useful to the common peace. But when the followers of Jesus become living demonstrations of opposition to the popular idols, the systems of injustice, the corrosive influence of greed, and the destructive policies of government, then the world's disagreement with the Christian community grows into hatred and violence.

THE CONTEXT OF HOSTILITY IN PETER'S LETTER

The first letter of Peter was written to a church facing impending hostility by the state and the pagan culture in general. In it the apostle reminded the community that the world's hostility was to be expected:

> *Dear friends, do not be surprised at the painful trial you*
> *are suffering, as though something strange were happening*
> *to you. But rejoice that you participate in the sufferings*
> *of Christ, so that you may be overjoyed when his glory is*
> *revealed. If you are insulted because of the name of*
> *Christ, you are blessed, for the Spirit of glory and of*
> *God rests on you.*[5]

Why should this be so? Because the Christian community is an alternative way of thinking and living. It is a counterculture. It marches to a different drummer. It worships only one God, who is altogether holy and righteous and just and merciful. It lives as the community of Light. This is *evangelism.* As Peter said:

> *Dear friends, I urge you, as aliens and strangers in the*
> *world, to abstain from sinful desires,*[6] *which war against*
> *your soul. Live such good lives among the pagans that,*
> *though they accuse you of doing wrong, they may see your*
> good deeds *and glorify God on the day he visits us.*
> (emphasis added)[7]

The gospel is visible in a different kind of community. That community smells like Christ; its residents have the aroma of Christ. The Holy Spirit is going before, in, and through this community to enable outsiders to see God at work in New Creation. What happens next? The evangelistic process continues as the Holy Spirit makes these outsiders curious—so curious that they ask questions. Again, listen to Peter:

> *Who is going to harm you if you are eager to do good? But even if you should suffer for what is right, you are blessed. "Do not fear what they fear; do not be frightened." But in your hearts set apart Christ as Lord. Always be prepared to give an answer to everyone who asks you to give the reason for the hope that you have. But do this with gentleness and respect, keeping a clear conscience.*[8]

The followers of Christ live differently. They are a wonderful, wholesome, enviable New Creation. They elicit curiosity. On the one hand, they demonstrate contagious compassion. On the other, they give themselves joyously to God. They worship. They have hope and meaning and love. Outsiders ask questions. Insiders (believers) listen to their questions and invite them in for coffee, then gently and respectfully explain that it is Jesus who has recreated their lives, that the Holy Spirit is at work. These outsiders (whom the Bible often calls *pagans*) may or may not respond immediately, but the seed has been sown. The followers of Christ have been faithful.

Still, when the followers of Jesus, with their zeal for justice and mercy, order their lives according to the principles of the Dominion of God, and when this becomes a threat, the *powers* may well retaliate. People may be set free in Christ. New life may be spurting out of every unexpected place. Joy like a river may be flowing in the community of faith. But all hell may be breaking loose at the same time! *"Don't think it strange . . ."*

INCARNATIONAL THROUGH AND THROUGH_____

Jesus, who lives in and with his followers, is also their model for such *holistic* evangelism. He came into his own creation, but in its rebellion it did not receive him. Yet, he had been sent by the Father for the specific mission of accomplishing that which opened the door into God's redemption. This total self-awareness made him completely free in whatever place or confrontation he found himself. In his private prayers he agonized with his Father over specific implementations of this calling, but there was never any doubt as to who he was or why he had come. Even at the climax of the Cross he could utter the statement of accomplishment: "It is finished!"

The first principle of holistic evangelism, then, is to "sanctify the Lord always in your hearts" or to be certain that by repentance and faith you have embraced Jesus. It is to know and embrace the *data,* the *demands,* and the *promises* of the gospel. It is to be *free to be the followers of Christ.* This is the import of John's word: "Yet to all who received him, to those who believed in his name, he gave the right to become children of God."[9] Followers of Christ find deep meaning in their identity with Jesus and with the mission of God. Each life is significant in history because it is part of God's plan. This deep resonance gives songs in the night!

Remember too that as Jesus lives in us by the power of his resurrection, by the power of the Holy Spirit, then what was true of Jesus in his earthly life, in a very dynamic way, becomes true of us. As God's Spirit and Word formed the obedience of Jesus, so too with those of us who are his. The followers of Jesus spend their days in a morally and intellectually amorphous culture, but with a commitment to Truth as revealed by God in Christ. It is by this that the kingdom lifestyle is demonstrated in our lives. And it is quite subversive.

By his life and behavior, Jesus exhibited God's infinite compassion for his creation in *chaos.* Jesus reached out in love to the tragically lost men and women whom he met in his daily sojourn in homes and on dusty streets. So must we. He had mercy upon those who were victims of the darkness. So must we. Jesus has bestowed upon his followers the commission to demonstrate the same life and love for each other that he demonstrated toward them. The Christian community is to be a demonstration of the radical love and grace of God in Jesus Christ.

Incarnation in an Alien Context

Jesus lived and ministered the mission of God in the midst of a religious and political context that had a totally different agenda than the one he was declaring. The Roman government; the Jewish establishment; the other world religions; the political, economic, and social powers found his teachings troublesome. His execution was not because he loved and did good works. It was his teachings, so subversive to all they stood for, that perpetrated his Cross. The lesson for his followers is that his faithfulness to his mission became the triumph over the very powers that sought to destroy him. Jesus also tapped into a profoundly deeper spring of joy, which enabled him to endure! He was faithful even unto death. That also is part of the evangelistic mandate!

Our daily incarnation is among real persons, real neighborhoods, a real *polis* (or political structure), a real culture with its myriad subcultures, real intellectual crosscurrents, real powers. All of these realities do not fit neatly into trite axioms. Indeed, the pilgrimage into faith never follows clever formulae. But the Spirit of God can use tragedies, doubts, struggles, ambiguities, and dark nights of the soul to bring men and women into the household of God. The church's faithful witness to Christ by preaching and daily conversation is all a part of that mysterious working.

Our incarnation is in a vastly troubled world, but in a world which is God's creation and which he loves. This *hope* is also part of our gospel and one of the deep springs into which we tap in the midst of pain and tears. The message of *hope* is essential to the gospel of the kingdom.

Cultural Collapse at the Beginning of a New Century

Over these past centuries there has been an accommodation with the world which is designated *Christendom*. In this accommodation the

Subversive Jesus, Radical Grace

Christian community was given much privilege and freedom. Here at the beginning of the twenty-first century Christendom is collapsing. So also is the whole cultural structure of the Enlightenment that has been so much a part of our Western culture since the eighteenth century: rationality (Descartes), the scientific method (Bacon), and human dignity and rights in politics (Locke).

The idols of North American individualism are producing bitter fruits as the environment is spoiled, as politics become captive to economic powers, as individual rights run rampant at the expense of responsibility to the larger community. Decadent Christianity devolves into affinity for pagan spirituality. The antagonistic culture revolts against Christian hegemony in social institutions with bitterness and scorn. Militant "Christian" groups display a frightening biblical-Christian illiteracy and an indifference to major teachings of Jesus. This means that the context of our ministry of the gospel finds confusion without and within the church. There are tears and pain in following Christ.

But Jesus Walks the Hell with Us and Shows Us the Way

That this is at the very heart of the New Testament teachings is obvious. It has nowhere, to my mind, been stated more poignantly than in Ernest Gordon's account of his captivity in the Japanese prison camp in the Kwai River valley in the jungles of Southeast Asia during World War II. In the midst of horrific and dehumanizing conditions, a British country lad became the point of gospel entrance when he smuggled a tattered New Testament into the camp in his loin-cloth. At the nadir of human hopelessness, this young man and his simple love for Jesus, demonstrated in servanthood, became the means by which cynical prisoners began to listen to and study God's Word. What emerged was a vital Christian community in this prison camp; New Creation in the context of all that was wrong and filled with the stench of death. Ernest Gordon, the regimental commander, was constrained to be the teacher of these Scriptures simply because he was the only one who had been to the university. He professed to be agnostic, but the

Spirit of God worked in him along with the rest.

At the end of his account of this remarkable and transformational occurrence, he summarizes:

He [Christ] had opened me to life and life to me.
   In the prison camp we had discovered nothing new.
The grace we had experienced is the same in every
generation and must ever be received afresh.
   The good news for man is that God, in Christ, has shared
his suffering; for that is what God is like. He has not shunned
the responsibility of freedom. He shares in the saddest and most
painful experiences of his children, even that experience which
seems to defeat us all, death itself.
   He comes into our Death House to lead us through it.[10]

TWO REAL AND PRESENT DOMINIONS

Too often our confusion comes from misinterpreting the teachings of the New Testament about two distinct and clashing kingdoms: the kingdom of God and the kingdom of Satan. The New Testament documents are quite clear about the reality of the powers of darkness that energize this world in rebellion. The prince of darkness comes as seducer, as an angel of light, as a destroyer and liar, given supernatural (though limited) power.[11] It is into this context of the dominion of darkness that Jesus comes boldly announcing and inaugurating a new and eternal dominion, the Dominion of God. This new reality is the fulfillment of the prophecies of the New Covenant. It is an *already-but-not-yet* kingdom. It is present and dynamic but not yet consummated. And this means that between the first coming of Christ and his return at the end of the age, we all live in the presence of two very real dominions.

By our baptism into Christ, we who are his followers have renounced the darkness and identified with the Son of God. We have embraced him and been marked by his Cross. But the rebellious cosmos, the *hell*, the dominion of darkness, is still the context in which we operate. We do not, then, stand or sit idly by and wait for Jesus to return. We become the practitioners, the missioners, of New Creation right in the midst of, and often bearing the antagonism of, the old and rebellious creation. It is after all, our Father's world. But we are only *more than conquerors* in the midst of (not isolated from) the pain and death and hardship that we face from it.

A facet of our evangelistic obedience is the realization that our presence in the world is all that gives it meaning and preserves it from total destruction. We are, after all, *salt and light.* We are God's instruments of righteousness in a context of unrighteousness. This also is evangelism.

BACK TO THE SECOND CENTURY _____

Throughout this book we have sought to bring fresh understanding to the work of evangelism. The task before us is that of *making disciples* among all people-groups and in the alien cultural context of the world. Especially do we have in mind here our friend Chip and Generations X and Y (as well as the Millennial Generation, which comes along next). Communicating the indescribably good message of Jesus is going to be effective in such a culture primarily by the demonstration of New Creation in the *lives* of the followers of Jesus more so than by the use of words.

It is typical of North Americans to put confidence in the use of words, in pulpit oratory, or in sales techniques to persuade people, and certainly the verbal declaration of Christ is an integral part of evangelistic faithfulness. But it can be vacuous if not accompanied by the demonstration of transformed lives and transformed community. The current culture of sullenness and hyperactivity can easily blow off words and hustles. The rapid paganization of North American culture has brought us back to the situation in which our second-century counterparts found themselves. Indeed, a document from that era, *The Letter to Diognetus,* is instructive for our purposes here:

> For Christians are not differentiated from other people
> by country, language, or customs; you see, they do not

live in cities of their own, or speak some strange dialect, or have some peculiar lifestyle.

This teaching of theirs has not been contrived by the invention and speculation of inquisitive men; nor are they propagating mere human teaching as some people do. They live in both Greek and foreign cities, wherever chance has put them. They follow local customs in clothing, food, and other aspects of life. But at the same time, they demonstrate to us the wonderful and certainly unusual form of their own citizenship.

They live in their own native lands, but as aliens; as citizens they share all things with others, but like aliens, suffer all things. Every foreign country is to them as their native country, and every native land as a foreign country.

They marry and have children just like everyone else, but they do not kill unwanted babies. They offer a shared table, but not a shared bed. They are at present "in the flesh" but they do not live "according to the flesh." They are passing their days on earth, but are citizens of heaven. They obey the appointed laws and go beyond the laws in their own lives.

They love everyone, but are persecuted by all. They are unknown and condemned; they are put to death and gain life. They are poor and yet make many rich. They are short of everything and yet have plenty of all things. They are dishonored and yet gain glory through dishonor.

Their names are blackened and yet they are cleared. They are mocked and bless in return. They are treated outrageously and behave respectfully to others. When they do good, they are punished as evildoers; when punished, they rejoice as if being given new life. They are attacked by Jews as aliens, and are persecuted by Greeks; yet those who hate them cannot give any reason for their hostility.

To put it simply — the soul is to the body as Christians are to the world. The soul is spread through all

Subversive Jesus, Radical Grace

parts of the body and Christians through all the cities of the world. The soul is in the body but is not of the body; Christians are in the world but not of the world.[12]

So it is that Jesus and the people of Jesus come into this rebellious and confusing creation as God's redemptively subversive New Creation. Our confidence is in the unlimited and outrageously radical grace of the God whose world it is, and whose love for it surpasses knowledge. The New Testament gospel of the kingdom of God cannot be marketed as a success formula, nor can we hold out the promises that people want to hear. Rather, our faithfulness is to demonstrate a life that sees the humanly unbridgeable difference between *chaos* and God's *Shalom*.

What we can offer to Chip and his generation is our demonstration of such New Creation lives, and be available and genuine in our communication and love.

"TOO WILD AND FREE FOR THE TIMID"

Such a Person as we embrace, such a message as forms us, is so absolutely unthinkable by those still outside. The conflict between the Beast and the Lamb portrayed in the last book of the Bible is ongoing and often causes us to cry out with our brothers and sisters: "How long, O Lord?" It is not a message that makes sense to the cynics. A wonderful Christian author related how unwilling her colleagues in the literary fraternity were to enter into any kind of a thoughtful engagement on the subject of Jesus Christ. Her conclusion was that "Jesus is too wild and free for the timid!"

Such is our faith.

As the cultural antipathy—the cultural darkness and hostility—grows around us, please remember that so does the sense of lostness, personal darkness, and spiritual hungering in the emerging generation who has no hope of their own. These are real. The Holy Spirit of the Risen Lord is not passive in the midst of this dark confusion; the infinite love and the radical grace of our Redeemer God is irresistibly at work in and through us, not to mention going before us!

In the midst of the most unspeakable agonies, Jesus walks with us in a way that surpasses human understanding, and we share with him the deep rivers of God's meaning, and of God's love, and of God's hope. The darkness becomes light, and God gives to his own such songs and such laughter as those outside can never imagine. It is to this evangelistic pilgrimage that Jesus calls us to be faithful. It is in the midst of the realities of this twenty-first century, and this new generational culture, that God calls us to be voices of hope and of gospel; to introduce Chip and his peers to God's great *Shalom*.

Shalom!

Notes

Preface

1. Jacques Ellul, *The Subversion of Christianity* (Grand Rapids, MI: Eerdmans, 1986). Ellul spells this out in detail in this work.
2. Matthew 28:20.
3. Luke 6:47, paraphrase.
4. Luke 24:47, paraphrase.
5. 1 Corinthians 15:24-26,28.

Chapter One

1. John 7:7.
2. Matthew 16:24.

Chapter Two

1. Westminster Larger Catechism, Question #1.
2. Psalm 19:1.
3. Romans 1:19-20.
4. Note that in a very real sense Scripture is also a part of our very good news! The God who wills to be known has spoken, and that which he has made known is somehow communicated to us down through the ages in the pages of Holy Scripture. God is not silent! But Scripture is also accepted on our part, and the church's part, as an act of faith. We are candid that this also is part of our faith assumption.
5. Mark 1:14.
6. Genesis 1:1; John 1:1-3.
7. The implications of the "Big Bang" theory of the origin of the universe are fascinating when compared here!
8. This word *Shalom,* which I shall use with a capital "S," is the Hebrew word which embraces the concepts of peace, harmony, beauty, balance, place, fulfillment, and a wholeness that is God's design for his creation. The Christian gospel is also referred to as the "gospel of peace" (Ephesians 6:15).

9. Compare C. S. Lewis, *The Lion, the Witch, and the Wardrobe* (New York: Macmillan, 1950), chapter fifteen.
10. Compare Genesis 3:15.
11. Compare Genesis 3:15.
12. Craig Barnes, *When God Interrupts* (Downers Grove, IL: InterVarsity, 1996), p. 60.
13. Exodus 19:6.
14. 2 Chronicles 7:14.
15. This is the basic content of the book of Deuteronomy.
16. Compare Deuteronomy 4.
17. Isaiah 58:6-12; Micah 6:8; Amos 5:24.
18. Isaiah 28:19.
19. Jeremiah 31:31-34; Ezekiel 36:24-32.
20. Jeremiah 29:11.
21. Zephaniah 3:17, paraphrased.
22. Isaiah 54:10, paraphrased.
23. Isaiah 42:1,4, paraphrased.
24. Isaiah 53:1-5, paraphrased.
25. Isaiah 61:1-2.
26. Compare Herman Ridderbos, *The Coming of the Kingdom* (Philadelphia: Presbyterian and Reformed Publishing Co., 1962), p. 8ff.
27. Barnes, p. 135.

Chapter Three

1. Ephesians 2:2, paraphrased.
2. The very nature of Hebrew literature is more poetic than our Western traditions, and whoever this figure is and how he arrived on the scene is not the point here. The fact that he is and that he continues to intrude himself right through the Bible until his ultimate destruction in Revelation is relevant. I leave it there. He is always portrayed as the destructive, untruthful, deceptive, slanderous, accusing figure who somehow energizes evil.
3. Romans 8:22, paraphrased.
4. Psalm 16:11, paraphrased.
5. Unknown twentieth-century poet.
6. John 8:33, paraphrased.
7. Ephesians 2:12.
8. From the title of a book by Walker Percy that is most provocative in portraying the quest after meaning in human existence. It doesn't fit any category of literature that I know. Its subtitle is: *The Last Self-Help Book You'll Ever Need.*
9. C. S. Lewis, *The Great Divorce* (New York: Macmillan, 1946).

10. From the writings of William Stringfellow. Stringfellow proposed that principalities and powers could be the national government, the company, the lodge or labor union, a college, or, alas, even the church!

11. Isaiah made the contrast between Jerusalem as the City of Shalom, and Jerusalem as the unfaithful city, which had become the city without meaning (compare Isaiah 24:10). This is very descriptive of American cities!

12. Jeremiah 29:7, paraphrased.

13. Compare Lesslie Newbigin, *The Gospel in a Pluralist Society* (Grand Rapids, MI: Eerdmans, 1960), p. 222: "The church is nothing other than that movement launched into the public life of the world by its sovereign Lord to continue that which he came to do. . . . It is bound to challenge in the name of the Lord all the powers, ideologies, myths, assumptions, and worldviews which do not acknowledge him as Lord."

14. Matthew 6:13; 1 John 5:19, paraphrased.

15. Revelation 12:10.

16. Acts 26:18, paraphrased.

17. Matthew 25:31-33.

18. *UTNE Reader,* November-December 1998, p. 45. An interview reveals Barbara Ehrenreich as a marvelously gifted but very secular person and author whose agenda includes a passion for issues and justice and environmental concern, which ought to be those of every citizen of the kingdom of God (but too often are tragically ignored).

19. John 3:17, paraphrased.

20. Genesis 18:18, paraphrased.

21. John 3:18, paraphrased.

22. 2 Corinthians 5:10, paraphrased.

23. Revelation 1:14, paraphrased.

24. Compare 1 Corinthians 3:15, which is written not to unbelievers but believers.

25. This is not a new struggle for the Christian church. It goes back to the earliest centuries. The Roman Catholic concept of purgatory is an idea of punishment for the temporal sins of believers. The idea of something beyond the infinite fire of judgment is not a guarantee on which we can build a doctrine. Likewise, the idea that all who resist God simply are terminated has received dubious reviews in the evangelical community. But this doesn't allow us to escape our meeting with God! This may also give a clue to the enigmatic reference to being baptized for the dead (1 Corinthians 15:29) and to the genesis of some parts of the church that regularly include prayers for the dead. Mystery!

26. Psalm 7:11.

27. Psalm 104:35; Isaiah 66:24; Psalm 9:11; Romans 6:23; Matthew 25:41; Revelation 20:15; 2 Thessalonians 1:6-8.

28. Compare Leon Morris, *The Apostolic Preaching of the Cross* (Grand Rapids, MI: Eerdmans, 1960), pp. 125-185.

29. Micah 7:18; Romans 11:15; 2 Corinthians 5:19; 1 John 2:2; Revelation 21; Revelation 20:14.

30. Anonymous, *The Best of Studdert-Kennedy: Selections from Writings by a Friend* (New York: Harper and Brothers, 1924, 1927, 1929), p. 160.

31. Compare Colossians 1:15-18.

32. Hebrews 12:2.

33. Quoted from C. S. Lewis, *Surprised by Joy,* in *C. S. Lewis: A Biography* by Roger Lancelyn Green and Walter Hooper (New York: Harcourt Brace Jovanovich, 1974), p. 103.

34. Genesis 18:25.

Chapter Four

1. The rage of Nirvana or the despair of Alanis Morissette say worlds about the existential *chaos* behind this music. Morissette's song "All I Want" talks about being consumed by "the chill of the solitary" and her desire to find a soul mate. Some of the most eloquent expressions of lostness and hopelessness can be found in such music, and in the writings of such spokespersons as Doug Copeland in his *Life After God.* Philosopher Richard Mouw poignantly sets in juxtaposition the lament of Mick Jagger in the Rolling Stones' familiar lyrics, "I can't get no satisfaction" against the Psalter version of "As the deer pants for living waters, so my soul thirsts for thee, O God."

2. A study a few years ago showed that most spontaneous evangelism was done by those who had been Christians for less than a year. The newly converted still remember their own lostness, still have friends who are outside, and are still thrilled by their discovery of Christ and want to share it. There is an irony here. One would think that the longer a person lived with the reality of God's love, the more likely he or she would be to seek occasions to make it known to others. The fact is that far too many Christians spend all their spare time with other Christians and so lose contact with the Chips of this world!

3. *UTNE Reader,* July-August 1998. This issue carried a series of articles under the rubric, "Designer God in a Mix and Match World, Why Not Create Your Own Religion?" The articles were a mix of philosophical and religious syncretism, an amalgam of legitimate longings and purely subjective solutions.

4. Psalm 10:4.

5. John 20:21.

6. Matthew 9:13; Luke 7:33-34; 19:10.
7. C. S. Lewis, *Weight of Glory* (New York: Collier, 1975), p. 19.
8. Ephesians 2:12.

Chapter Five
1. Attributed to D. T. Niles.
2. John 14:15; Matthew 8:24; 16:24; John 13:34.
3. Matthew 10:39.
4. Romans 8:29.
5. John 8:36.
6. Mark 1:14-15, paraphrased.
7. Matthew 24:14, paraphrased, emphasis added.
8. Luke 24:44-47.
9. I covered this expectation in chapter two when I talked about the coming of an Anointed Servant.
10. Isaiah 49:6.
11. Isaiah 59:14-20.
12. Isaiah 61:1-3.
13. Isaiah 58:6-7.
14. Isaiah 53:5.
15. If this sounds strange to our understanding of what *salvation* involves, consider that when the apostle Paul was spelling out for the readers in Rome what the transformed life offered to God would look like, he echoed these same prophetic and Sermon on the Mount themes. Compare Romans 12:9-21.
16. Luke 1:32-33.
17. Luke 1:46,51-55, paraphrased.
18. Luke 4:21, paraphrased.
19. The more accurate answers to these questions need to be addressed in the light of first-century Judaism, or Second Temple Judaism. Lucid expositions of this have been done by N. T. Wright, *(Jesus and the Victory of God)*, and Kenneth Bailey, *(Poet and Peasant Through Peasant Eyes)*.
20. Compare David J. Bosch, *Transforming Mission: Paradigm Shifts in Theology of Mission* (Marynoll, New York: Orbis Books, 1991), pp. 98-99, on these texts as a case in point.
21. Donald Kraybill, *The Upside-Down Kingdom* (Scottdale, PA: Herald, 1973), a most helpful guide to my thinking.
22. Romans 8:29.
23. Matthew 5:11-12.
24. Jacques Ellul uses this term in describing the "subversion of Christianity" in a volume by that title.

25. Matthew 7:13-14.

26. Acts 17:30; Mark 1:15.

27. Romans 16:26; 2 Thessalonians 1:8.

28. Ephesians 2:10.

29. 1 Peter 2:9.

Chapter Six

1. 1 Corinthians 1:21.

2. "And it is the Cross, more than anything else, that has called me inexorably to Christ." So said Malcolm Muggeridge in *A Twentieth-Century Testimony* (Nashville: Thomas Nelson, 1978), p. 72.

3. Luke 1:50-55.

4. Luke 4:18-19.

5. Isaiah 29:11-13.

6. This colorful designation for the priests and Levites is used by Walter Brueggemann in his helpful descriptions of temple culture.

7. Compare Andrew Purves, "The Lordship of Jesus Christ and the Christian Doctrine of the Trinity," in *reFORM,* Vol. 1, No. 1, p. 10.

8. See Leviticus 17:11 and Hebrews 9:22.

9. Isaiah 53:1-5.

10. Isaiah 53:6, 10–11, paraphrased.

11. Matthew 1:21,23.

12. Luke 1:30-33.

13. John 1:29.

14. John 10:17-18.

15. 2 Corinthians 5:21.

16. John 3:16-17.

17. Luke 24:44,46-47.

18. C. S. Lewis, *The Lion, the Witch, and the Wardrobe* (New York: Macmillan, 1950), chapter fifteen.

19. Colossians 2:15, NEB.

20. When one paints such a dark picture of what sin has caused in the personal, natural, and social realms, one must also factor in that reality, which the church has called "common grace," by which God in love keeps his creation from total self-destruction, by which he brings rain upon the just and unjust, by which he enables men and women who don't acknowledge him to do good works and produce works of art, justice, mercy, humanitarian goodness, and the like. But note, this also is undeserved and is therefore *grace*.

21. Lyrics to the hymn, "This Is My Father's World," by Maltbie Babcock.

Chapter Seven

1. This is stated beautifully in the hymn lyrics: "I sought the Lord, and afterward I knew He moved my soul to seek Him, seeking me: It was not I that found, O Savior true; No, I was found of Thee" (Pilgrim Hymnal).
2. The title of a popular gospel tract a few years back.
3. 2 Corinthians 4:4.
4. Acts 26:17-18.
5. Colossians 1:6,13, paraphrased.
6. It was such persons that the short-lived Pope, John Paul I, had in mind when he stated that the task of the church today was to "evangelize those already baptized."
7. Titus 3:4-5, paraphrased.
8. John 15:5.
9. John 10:7-9, paraphrased.
10. 2 Peter 1:3, paraphrased.
11. Matthew 6:33, paraphrased.
12. Ephesians 5:27.
13. Compare Acts 20:21.
14. John 15:7, paraphrased.
15. Romans 8:29.
16. Ephesians 4:24.
17. Colossians 3:10.
18. Galatians 4:19, emphasis added.
19. John 8:31-32.
20. Compare John 20:22; Acts 1:8.
21. Ephesians 1:19-20, *Good News for Modern Man*
22. John 14:15-24.
23. Ephesians 3:20-21, emphasis added.
24. 2 Corinthians 3:17-18.
25. John 14:13.
26. Mark 1:15; Acts 17:30.
27. Romans 6:1-15, paraphrased.
28. This rendering is from *The Book of Common Prayer* of the Episcopal Church. It is probably even more pointed in the more ancient renderings but contains essentially the same thrust.
29. 1 Peter 2:22.

Chapter Eight

1. I would especially recommend Jimmy Long, *Generating Hope* (Downers Grove, Ill.: Moody Press, 1997), p. X. Note chapter five, "Adopted Out of Shame into God's Family," as a most provocative explication of this point of the gospel.

2. Compare chapter three.
3. To Christians who are products of the modern era, such emphasis on "experience" sounds unacceptable, but to the postmoderns, and Xers such as Chip, this is critical. If it can't be experienced, it isn't worth much. Linear reasoning or Aristotelian logic, which has been the church's approach to so much of its presentation to the world for these past centuries, is replaced by a much more circular kind of reasoning that includes the experiencing of a thing. I offer this only because this is a book on the evangelistic mandate of the church, and this cultural reality is right on our doorstep. It is not altogether unbiblical either! Just frequently overlooked.
4. 1 Corinthians 2:4.
5. Through its Holy Congregation for the Purity of the Faith, the Roman Church, though rightly concerned for the purity of Christian teaching, used the weapons of the dominion of darkness to accomplish its ends. In the course of these inquisitions, many were persecuted whose ideas were not so much erroneous as they were fresh and creative insights into biblical teachings!
6. The Creed of Nicea from the Council of Nicea, A.D. 325.
7. 2 Corinthians 2:14-15.
8. Ephesians 3:21.
9. Revelation 15:3.
10. Colossians 1:15-20.
11. 2 Corinthians 3:18; 4:6.
12. Compare 1 Corinthians 2:16.
13. Romans 6 is a lucid explication of this.
14. Try "American interests abroad" for an idol that is enormously destructive!
15. 1 Peter 4:12-14.

Chapter Nine
1. John 14:18 (compare chapters 14–16).
2. Jeremiah 31:31-34; Ezekiel 36:24-33.
3. John 3:1.
4. Exodus 19:6.
5. Ephesians 3:20-21, emphasis added.
6. John 20:21, paraphrased.
7. Compare Colossians 3:12 in the J. B. Phillips paraphrase for light on this rendering.
8. Matthew 6:33, paraphrased.
9. 2 Peter 3:9.
10. John 1:11-12, paraphrased.
11. Ephesians 2:1-10.

12. 2 Corinthians 4:7.

13. Anglican John Stott humorously commented on this passage one time by saying, "When you have a blind congregation and a weak preacher, you *do* have a problem, don't you?"

This wonderful description is from the title of a book by John Perkins.
1 Corinthians 4:20.

gue

in 15:19-20.

idn't know that when I accepted Christ I was trading one hell for her! Nobody told me that." These revealing words came from an n-American friend who found new life in Christ while living in a charged inner-city housing project and who ultimately became rnationally fruitful Christian leader. His words are revealing as we the last piece of this sojourn.

4:13.

te this I am also reading a biographical study of the late Dietrich ffer, who after challenging the Nazi government and its policies the church could not even receive a call to a church as pastor. kness retaliated from within the German church!

4:12-14.

rase, also translated "the lusts of the flesh," has to do with the of chaos with its self-absorbed individual and corporate lives. It ly that we are not to give in to the distorted lifestyle of the dom-cial order or the principalities and powers that form and control ty around us.

2:11-12.

:13-16.

2.

ordon, *Through the Valley of the Kwai* (New York: Harper and 62), p. 256.

ink, in his seminal three-volume work on this subject, Satan as "God's overzealous quality control agent." This is to the very problem of the purpose of Satan in God's design and
12. dominion in his creation. Interesting thesis!

in *Eerdman's Handbook to the History of Christianity* (Grand MI: Eerdmans, 1977), p. 69.

Author

ROBERT THORNTON HENDERSON serves as Director of Seminary Ministry for Presbyterians for Renewal. He is a graduate of Columbia Theological Seminary and Westminster Theological Seminary, and he served as a pastor for almost forty years. He is the author of *A Door of Hope: Spiritual Conflict in Pastoral Ministry, Joy to the World,* and *Beating the Churchgoing Blahs.* He lives in Tucker, Georgia with his wife, Betty.